TEACH YOURSELF TO

Meditate

in 10 SIMPLE LESSONS

TEACH YOURSELF TO
Meditate
in 10 SIMPLE LESSONS

*Discover
Relaxation and
Clarity of Mind
in Just Minutes
a Day*

Eric Harrison

Ulysses Press
Berkeley, California

Published by: Ulysses Press
P.O. Box 3440
Berkeley, CA 94703
www.ulyssespress.com

Library of Congress Control Number: 2001094715
ISBN: 1-56975-275-3

First published in 2000 by Judy Piatkus Publishers, Ltd.
Published in agreement with Piatkus Books

Printed in Canada by Transcontinental Printing

10 9 8 7 6 5 4 3 2 1

Editor: Richard Harris
Editorial and production staff: Claire Chun, Lily Chou, Marin Van Young
Indexer: Sayre Van Young
Design: Sarah Levin

Distributed in the United States by Publishers Group West

This book has been written and published strictly for informational purposes, and in no way should it be used as a substitute for consultation with your medical doctor or other health care professional. All facts in this book came from published trade books, self-published materials by experts, magazine articles, personal interviews, and the personal-practice experiences of the author or of authorities quoted or sources cited. You should not consider educational material herein to be the practice of medicine or to replace consultation with a physician or other medical practitioner. The author and publisher are providing you with information in this work so that you can have the knowledge and can choose, at your own risk, to act on that knowledge. The author and publisher also urge all readers to be aware of their health status and to consult health professionals before beginning any health program, including changes in dietary habits.

Contents

✻

How to Use This Book

✻

There are thousands of manmade rules about meditation. There are the "one-size-fits-all" schools, where everyone chants the same mantra, or meditates for fifteen minutes twice a day, or does some special exercise at 6 am or 4 pm.

There are also the special instructions—"breathe this way, left foot over right, eyes open, eyes closed, eyes half open and half closed, don't eat garlic or meat, thumb touching third finger, imagine a blue or white or gold light. . . ." All imply that the magic won't work unless you do it just right.

In contrast, there are the natural laws that really determine success. To meditate well, for example, you do need to pay attention and keep the mind from wandering. You also need to understand what you're trying to do and check if it's actually happening. Self-observation, tolerance, and a certain playfulness of spirit are also necessary.

I have taught thousands of people to meditate. This book contains all the instructions I give in my basic meditation course. My father was an educator who believed in "student-centered learning." Like him, I try to help people learn what they want to know. People need to find their individual way into meditation and shape it to their own purposes.

There are many ways you could use this book. If you're completely new to the subject, you'll probably read just to understand what it's all about. If you already know how to meditate, you can pick out useful ideas to enhance your practice. If you actually teach meditation yourself, or would like to do so, this book can be a resource or give you a structure to work on.

But if you want to learn to meditate, I suggest you read this book with big pauses. Read an exercise two or three times, then put the book down and do it. Try out as many exercises as you like while you read. For the best results, choose a favorite and practice it several times. You need to do a meditation at least four times over four days for it to go into long-term memory.

Some meditations are more useful than others. The first part of this book outlines five "bedrock" practices. These five, plus "mantra," are the most popular in the world. They are easy to do and combine well with other practices. For example, you could meditate on the breath while also listening to sounds or saying an affirmation. Or you could scan the body while doing a visualization.

Scattered through the book are dozens of "spot meditations." You can do these whenever an opportunity arises—at traffic lights, in lines, walking the dog or while doing housework. These are not designed to take you to the point of sleep. They just strip off the top 20 percent of tension and slow down the mental chatter. These are the most time-efficient practices I teach. Often they are short modified forms of the standard meditations.

While reading this book, you're quite likely to make one big mistake. Because the theory is easy to understand, you may assume you therefore know how to do it. It just doesn't work that way. You only get good at a skill by practicing it regularly no matter how simple it seems.

This book is a ready-made kit. You just add time. If you read this book and do a few exercises, you will know what meditation is and how to do it. If you invest fifteen minutes a day, five days a week over the next two months, you will be very pleased with your progress. For a total of ten hours practice, you can develop a skill that could benefit the rest of your life. Have fun with it!

Introduction

Meditation is a delightful and healthy thing to do. It brings out our natural instinct for stillness and clarity. By meditating, we relearn a skill often lost since childhood: the ability to relax at will and return to inner balance. When we de-stress and slow down, we know who we are and what we feel, and how to act intelligently in a less-than-intelligent world. I personally can't imagine anything more valuable.

Of course, we also have a strong instinct for stimulation and excitement, which is what fuels our multi-trillion-dollar consumer industries. When we overdo it, we pay a heavy price: agitation, exhaustion, confusion, depression and illness. We feel out of balance, physically and mentally, and out of touch with ourselves. If this goes on for too long, we age prematurely and die young. Overstimulation and stress are toxic in high doses.

The way to move back toward balance is surprisingly simple. I've taught meditation to five-year-old children and they get it. If we let go of our habitual mental busyness and do something simple—almost nothing at all—the body automatically relaxes and the mind becomes clear. If we do this regularly, the results can be almost miraculous.

How can we take a holiday from thought? How do we stop thinking about a dozen things at once? We can't blank our thoughts out or finish them off. However, just as antelopes can live safely in the company of lions, we can escape our thoughts at will. It just takes practice.

Being More Sensual

All we have to do is shift from thinking to sensing. Whenever we focus on the sensations of the present—sight, sound, smell, taste or touch—the other thoughts drop into the background. In that moment you truly taste the cake; where is your mind then? If you listened carefully to the surrounding sounds for just thirty seconds, your thoughts would weaken their grip, and the body would start to relax.

This is the secret formula: be sensual. Shepherd the mind into the sense world. Taste the coffee, enjoy the evening clouds, sense your own body as you walk or sit, become a connoisseur of the moment. Meditation is about focusing on pleasant or useful things.

Most of us know this instinctively. We often choose to relax by doing sensual activities: eating or drinking, listening to music, walking in the park. By doing so, we put our thoughts and worries backstage to some degree.

When I first explain this principle in class, I often see expressions of disbelief on the faces of my students. They know how chaotic their minds are. How could focusing on the breath possibly help? And yet, one meditation later, they are pleasantly surprised. Somehow, it does work. And with practice, it can work very well indeed.

Detaching from Thoughts

Meditation is simple, but our minds are not. Our biggest challenge is our mental hyperactivity, our habit of continually thinking about everything under the sun. So is it possible to blank it out, or slow it down, or think only about useful things? How do we relate our ongoing thoughts and emotions?

The bad news is that they don't just go away. This is one of the grim truths that all meditators realize, sooner or later. The good news is that we can emotionally disengage from them. We can develop an ability to "just watch" thoughts with detachment.

Meditation is based on two skills: *focusing* on a sensory object and *passively watching* other thoughts and sensations. They work hand in hand. Focusing helps us escape from thoughts, like taking a short holiday from them. And when we can't help but notice our thoughts, we learn to "just watch" them without engaging them.

Different Techniques, Same Instructions

We can say that meditation is any technique that relaxes the body and gets the mind clear. A clear mind, by the way, is not blank. It's just a mind that sees clearly, with a certain emotional detachment.

Though there seems to be thousands of different meditations with different goals, their basic instructions are much the same: "Focus on one thing, and watch other thoughts and sensations with detachment."

In any meditation, you are asked to focus on, or direct your attention to, something and avoid distractions. Christian and New Age practices often focus on God, or a beautiful idea or image. Buddhist and Hindu groups are more earthy and commonly emphasize the body and other sense objects.

Furthermore, you can change focus in a meditation, as you do when you go through a visualization sequence. Or you can multi-focus, by tuning into a few things simultaneously. At deeper stages, you can focus on your quality of mind or emotion, or a dream image or memory. But you do need to focus. It won't work if you let the mind drift or space out.

It's Good to Analyze Your Meditation

Many meditators see thinking as the enemy, and feel you shouldn't try to analyze the experience. Religious groups often encourage this mindless, semi-hypnotic attitude to make students dependent on them. I found even my own teachers unwilling to answer my questions. I would ask, "How does meditation work? What is going on when I feel this?" Their usual response was "Just do it and figure it out."

I found however that if I analyzed the process and discussed it with others, my meditation improved enormously. Though meditation is a non-verbal state, it is still useful to think about it and understand how it works. It isn't an ineffable mystery, or something magically transmitted by a guru from Tibet or India. Beautiful and powerful as it is, it can be explained in terms of mental and physical processes that any psychologist or doctor would feel comfortable with.

When I started to teach, I tried to explain the process as clearly as I could. The languages of biology and psychology come naturally to me. I am a rational, skeptical Westerner at heart, and I wanted my students to understand what they were doing. I became the teacher I wanted to meet thirty years ago.

How I Learned to Meditate

For the past fifteen years, teaching meditation has been my full-time occupation. (This doesn't stop people from asking me if I have a *real* job as well.) I have now taught some 15,000 people since 1987, most of whom have attended a seven-week course at the Perth Meditation Centre.

Full-time Western meditation teachers who are not monks or nuns are very rare. However, we do exist and I met my peers at three conferences in California in the 1990s. On that evidence, you can say we are typically in our forties or fifties (because it takes that long to get a handle on the mind). Most of us spent years on the hippie trail in Asia from the early '70s, and/or trained in a Buddhist or Hindu tradition. And there are almost as many female as male teachers.

My own life-pattern is fairly typical. At university in New Zealand, though I studied literature, I was more interested in psychology and philosophy. After graduating at twenty, I traveled through Asia for three or four years, encountering mind-expanding drugs on the way.

At that time, I became a self-taught meditator. At first I just used meditation to settle down when my mind was going wild. Then I used it to deliberately enjoy the beauty of my surroundings. When I was in Bali, or India or the Himalayas, I was really there. Finally, it helped me think clearly when I had to make important decisions.

I started formal training in 1975, doing ten-day retreats in the Burmese tradition. The first one I attended had a stunning effect on me. I knew I'd found my passion in life. I was seriously tempted to drop everything and wholeheartedly pursue meditation.

I persuaded myself that trying to balance a normal life with meditation was better, but I now think that was the worst decision I've ever made. It was not until 1983 that I started three years training with Western teachers in the Kagyu lineage of Tibetan Buddhism.

This resulted in a seven-month retreat in the South Island of New Zealand. For most of that time, I lived in a tiny unheated hut high on a mountainside in the Southern Alps. I saw no one all week, except for Wednesdays, when I would collect my next week's food and spend the night with my girlfriend in the adjacent hut.

At last I had the solitude and stillness I'd always craved. I sat (i.e., meditated) for about nine hours a day, starting about 3 am. I also did two hours of yoga, two hours walking, a little writing and reading, and the housekeeping. I could feel the old self dying and a new one emerging. It was an unstoppable process and all I had to do was watch.

They were the richest months of my life. Despite the inner dramas and occasional horrible patches, I was not bored for a minute. I found the mind is indescribably beautiful and smart if you stop trying to manipulate it. I seemed to be a natural hermit.

I could have stayed there much longer, but the cold got to me. The hut had huge windows and no insulation. When the first snowfalls came, it was freezing. After several days wearing all the clothing I owned, and often my sleeping bag as well, I knew I had to leave.

Reluctantly, I returned to my little farm in the sunny north. I was part of the "back-to-the-land" movement of the 1970s. For eight years I had built houses, tended bees, planted trees, grown fruit and vegetables and helped my friends do the same.

After my long retreat, that lifestyle no longer appealed to me. My teachers had said I now knew enough to teach meditation. There were few possibilities in New Zealand, so on my thirty-sixth birthday, I returned to Australia and ended up in Perth.

How I Became a Teacher

My first class was held in a local "learning center." We could hear the children in the nursery and people gossiping in the corridors as we tried to meditate. This is what is euphemistically called "meditation in daily life."

Perth needed a meditation teacher and my work grew rapidly. Initially I taught at civic centers, universities, schools, government offices, prisons and from my home. The surroundings were rarely satisfactory, so in 1990 I opened up the Perth Meditation Centre and persuaded people to come to me. Soon I was teaching about 1000 people a year.

The center was in West Perth, just a mile from the heart of the city. It overlooked Kings Park, 400 acres of magnificent bush land with escarpment views over the Swan River. People coming to classes would go up two flights of stairs, past the offices of Fairfax Newspapers and the Mineral Mapping Agency. The center itself occupied the whole top floor and was simply furnished, with jungles of vegetation in each corner.

The main teaching room was an unusually beautiful space to find in office-land. It was spacious and airy, with light and sky views coming through windows on three sides. It was very suitable for a class of twenty, though at times we squeezed in over a hundred people for talks and workshops.

In the mid-1990s, I was employing two other teachers and a secretary and still working seventy hours a week. My overhead was $100,000 a year. Then one of my wealthy students said to me, "With that overhead, no small businessman like you can sleep well at night." And he was right. I wasn't a good model for my students.

When the building was demolished in 1998, I moved to the café district of nearby Subiaco. I laid off my staff and reduced my classes and overhead. I started writing books again and took up golf.

I had descended from the mountains of New Zealand to the marketplace in Perth. Without consciously planning it, I realized this had always been my goal. Much as I loved my time in retreat, I found it too easy, being a natural introvert. For me, it was a greater psychological challenge to find a useful role in the everyday world.

Similarly I didn't want my students to feel that they had to escape to the woods to meditate. After a week or two of classes, they find themselves meditating well in an office block in a busy part of town. They gradually learn to do the same at home, amid the sounds of traffic outside and the kids down the hall.

Saying Goodbye to Buddhism

Like many Western teachers, I had an uneasy relationship with the Buddhist tradition I trained in. I loved its psychological insight and brilliant meditation practices but was very aware of its faults—its authoritarian, sexist and life-denying qualities, for example. I consciously kept my activities at Perth Meditation Centre as un-Buddhist as possible.

Yet for a decade I was involved in Buddhist groups and tried to be a modernizing influence within them. I gave workshops and lecture series on Buddhist themes. I personally sponsored the visits to Perth of non-monastic Western men and women from the Tibetan, Burmese and Zen traditions.

At first the visits seemed successful. Hundreds of people came and retreats were well-attended. But a disconcerting pattern soon emerged. Despite the innovative teaching, almost none of those students returned. They could feel the Old Time Religion behind the words.

My attempts to bring Buddhism into the 20th century had borne small fruit. I had learned a lot about the strength of tradition and my arrogance in trying to change it. I began to seriously question my involvement with Buddhism at all. At this time, I wrote my book, *The Naked Buddha—Demythologized Account of the Man and His Teaching*.

Finally, I realized that it was time to walk away from Buddhism. The techniques are superb, but the institutions are frozen in time, and the key ideas contain fatal flaws. For example, Buddhism denies the value of individuality and "soul," which I think is very bad psychology.

My passion for meditation took me deep into Asian culture, but eventually my ancestors called me home. I am inescapably a fair-skinned Westerner of Irish descent, steeped in the whole European tradition. The spirit of restless inquiry that we find in men like Socrates, Shakespeare and Darwin is in my bones. The idealism of the East, despite its charms, just can't compete.

Eric Harrison
Perth, Western Australia
November 2001

PART ONE

Why We Meditate

✳

Meditating for Better Health

✳

Don't be surprised if your doctor says to you, "Have you considered meditation?" He's not some alternative quack. Each year I teach about 200 people—a quarter of my intake—on doctors' referrals.

The doctors are on firm ground when they recommend meditation. They are backed up by hundreds, perhaps thousands, of scientific studies going back decades. I attended a medical conference recently where the doctor who spoke on meditation cited 212 references in his paper.

The jury has delivered its verdict. Meditation is not like the latest wonder herb from the Amazon. It's not a kind of faith healing based on hypnotic suggestion. If you are sick, meditation can help in measurable ways. If you are not sick, meditation will help you stay healthy. It works in two main ways: it helps the body relax quickly and it settles the overwrought mind.

Restoring Balance

Meditation works because it restores the body to a state of balance. This is technically called "homeostasis," in which the systems within the body are at rest or operating within sustainable limits. The muscle tone is just right; the heart and breathing rates are normal; the levels of gastric juices, blood sugar and acidity are within the ideal range, and so on.

The body is quite capable of operating outside the state of balance. We can run a marathon, for example, or eat a massive meal, without suffering unduly. However, we're stressing those systems in the body when this happens. If they stay stressed for too long, they get damaged and pathologies start to occur. In fact, sickness can be easily defined as a state of imbalance in one or more of the systems in the body.

The body is always striving to return to homeostasis. Not only do systems work best when in balance, but this is also the optimum state for self-repair and growth. The body puts away the groceries, tidies the house and does structural repairs only when we're relaxed during the day or asleep at night. By relaxing when we can during the day and de-stressing effectively at night, we help the body heal itself.

The Stress and Relaxation Responses

The role of maintaining balance falls on the autonomic nervous system. This operates via two opposing functions, which we can call the stress response and the relaxation response.

The stress response is like pushing the accelerator flat to the floor. We get a lot of speed but quickly run out of gas. Adrenaline is the main hormonal instigator. Our muscles tighten, blood pressure and breathing rates rise, digestion stops and we burn a lot of energy fast. This often feels good as long as it doesn't last too long.

During the relaxation response, the reverse happens. Adrenaline levels fade, muscles soften, blood pressure and breathing rates drop and digestion resumes. We return to balance and burn energy at a sustainable rate.

Our bodies are extremely good at maintaining balance, so why do we still unexpectedly get sick? In theory, we could be in a balanced state all day long—eating, working, exercising and resting well. If we kept this going all our lives, there is a good chance we would live to a hale and hearty old age.

But, being conscious animals, we frequently ignore the signs of stress and overrule the intelligence of our bodies. We get overexcited, push ourselves to the limits and lose all concept of a balanced life. Though we often grind to a halt out of exhaustion, we usually don't recover fully before plunging back into the fray.

We can also be mildly stressed for years at a time. Just to be 10 percent more stressed than we need to be can make us as prone to middle-aged illness as periodic extreme stress. Because mild continual stress is so common, we take it as "normal" and don't realize how insidious it is.

The Effects of Chronic Stress

Stress affects every system of the body, pushing it beyond the level of sustainable function. High blood pressure leads to heart disease and kidney and respiratory failure. High metabolic rates lead to fatigue and cell damage. Muscular tension leads to physical pain and injury and poor circulation. Constricted respiration contributes to asthma and the lung infections that commonly take away the elderly. The disruption to the digestive system leads to a range of gastrointestinal problems.

The immune system in particular suffers when under stress, and a poor immune system affects everything. Many diseases seem particularly related to the malfunctioning of the immune system. It is not surprising that stressed people succumb to illnesses that healthy people shrug off lightly. Years of inner warfare have destroyed their defense capabilities.

Within minutes, meditation can temporarily reverse many of the indicators above. While you meditate, you're lowering blood pressure and breathing rates, muscle tension, adrenaline production and so.

This can be very beneficial for certain illnesses. Meditation has the most dramatic effects on people suffering from hypertension, insomnia, migraines, chronic pain and digestive and respiratory problems. While it occasionally acts as a miracle cure for a specific illness, it is more valuable in improving total body health. Let me explain how meditation affects the different systems in the body.

The Cardiovascular System

With some ailments such as cancer, the links between stress and health are somewhat indirect. With cardiovascular problems, however, the dynamics are obvious and the links are clear: stress is a major contributor to heart disease.

The stress response is designed to massively increase the available energy in the bloodstream in preparation for fight-or-flight. The cardiovascular system is the main engine and delivery system for this.

When stressed, the blood becomes thick with energy-laden fatty acids and glycogen. To deliver these to the muscles more rapidly, the heart and breathing rates increase and the veins and arteries constrict. The accelerated heart is now pumping a more viscous fluid through narrower passages much faster than usual.

This alone can kill you if you're vulnerable. In a stroke or heart attack, the blood vessels burst under the sheer pressure. A sudden spike of extreme fear, anger or terror can kill you on the spot.

The real damage, however, occurs over years. Increased pressure causes tiny rips in the lining of the arteries. The thicker blood carries semi-solid blobs of fatty acids within it which scour the walls and increase the damage. When damage occurs, blood platelets and fatty acids get under the lining, coagulate and seal the damage. However, each piece of repair work is bulky and juts into the passageways, making them narrower and increasing the overall pressure.

The scene is now set for real damage. A clot will often break loose under pressure and block a small arteriole. Within seconds, all the cells downstream will suffocate and die. These "micro-deaths" or "infarcts" are common in older people but can happen in any of us. Of course, if a large clot breaks loose and jams a major artery, we have a heart attack or stroke.

Heart attacks are dramatic, but the real culprit is years of hypertension, which day by day degrades the cardiovascular system. So what can you do to help—besides diet, exercise and drugs? In brief, anything that helps you relax will deactivate the stress response and bring you back into balance. Quite simply, the more relaxed you are during the day, the more you care for your heart and arteries.

The Far-reaching Effects of a Tight Musculature

The benefits of a supple musculature are almost impossible to over-estimate. The muscles of a healthy child are soft, supple and strong. The ability of muscles to expand and contract fully, as they do in a child, is the epitome of good health. Every cell in the body benefits from healthy muscle function.

Chronically tight muscles burn a lot of energy to stay tight, so they get fatigued and we underuse them. Being stiff, they're prone to injury and many of us carry dozens of micro-injuries in places like the lower back.

Healthy muscles are well-aerated and supplied with nutrients, because they relax and contract many times a day. In contrast, tight muscles clamp down on the tiny passageways that carry the blood. The tightest parts of a muscle are like a fortified city. When the gates are closed, supplies can't get in and waste products can't get out. The muscle is starved of oxygen and nutrients and poisoned by its own waste products. Such muscles eventually atrophy and die.

It's not just the muscles that suffer. If the thousands of little muscles throughout the body are tight, they impede the flow of oxygen and nutrients through the veins and arteries. This means that *all* the organs of the body, not just the muscles themselves, can suffer from reduced rations. If you are fighting a disease, a tense body is cutting off the supply lines.

Tight muscles also magnify the effects of stress on breathing and digestion. Both these systems operate on a rhythmic contraction and expansion of muscles. When muscles lock into contraction, these systems suffer.

So how does meditation help? It's very simple. Adrenaline raises muscle tone. It makes muscles contract. Meditating reduces adrenaline, and muscle tone fades. Thousands of big and small muscles throughout the body begin to soften within seconds of starting to meditate. It's not a mystery. If you feel your face or shoulder muscles starting to droop, you can be confident it's happening elsewhere as well.

The Upset Tummy

When the body goes into fight-or-flight mode, it switches off the digestion system. Secretions of saliva and digestive juices dry up and the muscles in the gut spasm and lock. The shop is closed. Nothing will move until the crisis is felt to have passed.

There is a good reason for this. The process of digestion itself consumes 10 to 20 percent of the body's available energy each day. In a perceived crisis, the mind says, "Digestion can wait. We need that energy for action," and it diverts the energy to the fight-or-flight muscles of the arms and legs.

Digestion will only start again when we relax. Unfortunately, we often stay tense for hours or days at a time. Since this is not an environment suited to digestion, we literally have "in-digestion," complete with flatulence and discomfort, and a quite accurate perception that food is sitting heavy in our bellies going nowhere.

Hundreds of studies have proven the connection between stress and the gut. Anxious people commonly suffer from ulcers, heartburn, gas, pain, diarrhea and/or constipation. Stress results in excess hydrochloric acid production and disturbs other digestive juices. If you get several of these symptoms regularly, you could say you have Irritable Bowel Syndrome.

One reason for constipation is that peristalsis is inhibited when we are stressed. Peristalsis is a soft, rhythmic expansion and contraction of gut muscles that squeezes food down the tract. When you're tense, however, the whole tubular system goes into contraction and nothing moves.

As soon as you meditate, you can feel yourself reversing this pattern. As you relax you may start salivating more. This is a clear sign that the digestive system is coming back to life. People often have to swallow at a certain point in their meditation. Another sign is a gurgling stomach. People who are constipated often find they are ready for a bowel movement after meditating.

The Immune Function under Stress

The body only repairs itself when you are relaxed during the day or asleep at night. Stress produces excess cortisol, which is a potent immunosuppressant. It also produces other indicators of reduced immune function that are too complex to detail here.

If you're chronically tense, your muscles will be deprived of oxygen and feel sore. The pervasive low-grade muscle pain that goes with stress makes people stiff in their movements and often physically inactive. This is disastrous for the lymphatic system.

The lymphatic system is an extensive network of tubes and glands that fights infection and removes waste products throughout the body. Unlike the cardiovascular system, it lacks a pump to drive it along. It is completely dependent on adjacent muscular activity to keep the lymph moving. People who are bedridden, for example, often have lymph pooling in their feet under the influence of gravity.

If the lymphatic system becomes stagnant through inactivity and rigid musculature, it is less capable of fighting disease and is vulnerable to being infected by the pathogens it is trying to destroy. People with cancers, for example, often need their diseased lymph glands removed as well.

Researchers have unfortunately done lots of experiments stressing little animals to death. From these we know how stress affects immune function. The thymus gland, the lymph glands and the spleen all shrink. The adrenal gland, working hard to pump out enough adrenaline, becomes enlarged. The white blood cell count drops.

The immune system is complex and difficult to understand. It's actually a range of semi-autonomous functions. Sometimes it breaks down because it's overvigilant and starts destroying healthy tissue, as in rheumatoid arthritis. At other times it becomes exhausted and unable to respond quickly enough to combat pathogens (the best time to destroy the enemy is the moment they first appear, before they can get a foothold).

The immune system is like a standing army constantly engaged in guerrilla warfare on the borders. It never rests. Like any army under constant pressure, it get exhausted, runs out of supplies, gets ambushed from behind and lacks time to regroup and consolidate. The epidemiological evidence supports what we know anyway: if you're stressed, you're much more vulnerable to quite mild pathogens like the flu. If this is the case, you'll also be struggling to cope with bigger problems.

The Roots of Fatigue

The biological purpose of the stress response is to give us energy to burn. All those muscles are wired up, burning a huge amount of energy that's going nowhere. A bricklayer enjoying his work will actually burn less energy than a chronic worrier who sits in a chair all day.

If we burn energy fast, we burn out. Stress and worry inevitably lead to exhaustion. And while we may collapse into sleep, we're unlikely to sleep well enough or long enough to recover fully. If we wake feeling awful and then plunge back into the stress zone, the cycle continues.

When young, this high energy/low energy cycle can be a character trait that is hard to break. Many young people are dazzlingly vivacious, running on caffeine and excitement, and often succeed in their careers because this is part of their self-image. It's who they think they are.

But as the high-energy hormones of youth start their inevitable decline sometime after thirty, such people wonder why they feel so tired all the time. Useful as nutritional supplements, exercise and other lifestyle factors are, they can't mask the underlying problem forever. Such people have been blowing the budget for years.

Meditation is sometimes described as energy conservation. By doing something simple (i.e., focusing), and watching thoughts rather than reacting to them, you save energy. We usually call this being relaxed. The more hours during the day that you're relaxed, the more energy you save.

Insomnia

If you're relaxed during the day, you also get maximum benefit from your sleep at night. If you fall asleep from sheer exhaustion, you're likely to be mentally turbulent during the night. People recognize this when they wake at two in the morning with their minds racing.

Meditation helps insomniacs in many ways. It detaches you from thinking before you go to sleep. If you meditate in bed, you'll usually go to sleep rapidly. If you wake in the night, you can detach from the thoughts that are keeping you awake. And even if you fail to fall asleep again, you can be relaxed in that state (i.e., conserving energy) rather than fretting (i.e., burning energy).

Sleep researchers are suggesting that maybe 90 percent of us, with the exception of the young and the elderly, are constantly sleep-deprived. If we want to be healthy, we could all do with more and better quality sleep.

My students often say they have their best sleeps on the night of their meditation class. It is sad, but many of us have to relearn how to sleep and to value our rest. Otherwise we face a lifetime of periodic exhaustion with its accompanying feelings of lethargy, helplessness and despair.

Living Comfortably with Pain

Some of my best students are those who suffer chronic pain. They have good motivation to practice and they see the results immediately. They commonly say meditation is the only thing that is guaranteed to work.

Pain usually has some injury at its base, but stress will enormously amplify the amount of pain you feel. Tense muscles ache because of oxygen deprivation and exhaustion. Since muscles are 40 percent of our body mass, this translates into pain all over the body and augments the pain of actual injuries.

If we're stressed, nothing in our body functions very well. It's not surprising that we have stomach pains, headaches and a susceptibility to niggling low-level infections that make us miserable.

Meditation helps immediately with pain because it cleans up our emotional response. Pain and emotion come hand in hand. Any pain we feel is a combination of the injury plus our emotional reaction to it. If we hate, fear or resent the pain, we project those emotions onto it and it feels much worse.

Meditation doesn't get rid of the pain or block it out. These are two impossible scenarios. Instead, it helps us to "just watch" the pain with detachment. The Stress Reduction Program at the University of Massachusetts has had phenomenal results in reducing a patient's perception of pain in this way. If the "pain" a person feels is 20 percent pure sensation and 80 percent emotional amplification, then watching the pain with detachment completely changes its character.

Anxiety, Panic and Phobias

Meditation is the perfect antidote to anxiety, panic and phobias. They are all the result of the stress response locked in overdrive. Meditation, as a way of consciously relaxing, disarms the stress response that causes the problem.

I often teach clients in conjunction with their psychologists or psychiatrists. Our work is beautifully complementary. They help their clients to a cognitive understanding of their problems, while I help them reverse the physical effects in their bodies. If our clients can wind their tension levels down from 90 percent of maximum to 70 percent, they are much less likely to suffer panic attacks or succumb to phobias. It has been very gratifying to see people extract themselves from states of extreme misery in this way.

As we age, we become less resilient to stress. Our stress levels typically build as the years go by. The rational worry that goes with living in a uncertain world spills over into toxic worry about things that don't matter or things we can't control. We try to cope with demanding situations by cranking up the energy. If we try really hard and work long hours, we feel safer than if we relax and take it easy. Our habitual tension level—the rate at which we burn energy—moves a few notches higher.

Before we realize it, we can be running very close to the panic mark all the time we are awake. A few years like this, usually in our twenties and thirties, seriously depletes our inner resources. All it takes is one extra outer stress and we're thrown over the line. We explode at the kids or take stress leave or fall ill or suffer a nervous breakdown.

Usually, we're flummoxed by the situation. Our strategy when under pressure has always been to push more, and we can see what that has led to. We can't just make some little adjustment and get back on track. It often requires a change in self-image and values and a willingness to listen compassionately to the needs of our body.

Helping with Chronic Illness

We occasionally hear of "miracle" cures through meditation, and there is little doubt they do occur. People boast, "Five years ago, the doctors gave me six months to live, but I'm still here." To be fair to doctors, they're usually quite accurate in their predictions, but they work on the law of averages. There will always be those at the extremes who unexpectedly recover from (or unexpectedly succumb to) illnesses.

So what was the secret of those who unexpectedly recover? This is notoriously hard to pin down, but they usually have a healthy and well-balanced optimism that doesn't slip into denial. Furthermore, they commonly take control of their treatment and make lifestyle changes to support the process.

Meditation can be a linchpin to these changes. At the very least, it helps us cope with pain and distress. It also helps us see the dramas around our illness with some detachment and emotional control.

Nonetheless, its direct physical benefits remain enormous. People with cancer often ask me, "How can I boost my immune system?" This question usually comes from the rather simplistic attitude that positive thoughts will help rally the troops.

Meditation acts in a more comprehensive way. The battle between the immune system and an illness is a drawn-out war of attrition, like World War Two. Victory goes to the side with greater industrial capacity and access to raw materials. The wins and losses occur on the front line, but the war is actually won in the factories and farms and scientific laboratories.

While meditation has specific effects on the immune system, its real benefits are much wider. Meditation will help you digest your food better, improve blood circulation and heart function, sleep better, cope with pain and distress better and enjoy life more despite your illness.

If your body as a whole is functioning in a healthy and relaxed manner, it's got the resources to fight a specific illness. Since meditation, with its ability to restore and maintain a general state of homeostasis, acts as the command post, this may be all you need to turn around a serious illness.

A Natural Psychotherapy

Meditation is obviously good for our health, but will it help with the mental pain that many of us suffer each day? And can it give us the states of extraordinary mental health and vigor described, for example, in the Asian literature? Is awakening or enlightenment or union with God really possible? Even people who meditate for panic attacks or insomnia feel that meditation can offer more than symptom relief.

Twenty-four hours a day, our bodies are working for self-repair and maximum function. They have a profound instinct for health. It seems that the mind has just the same passion for health and balance as the body. In fact, the process of mental healing is just as systematic and thorough as the way the body cleans up illnesses and repairs wounds.

The best way to support both physical and mental healing is to do nothing and watch. The body repairs itself best when we are relaxed or asleep. Similarly, the mind works best if we can just stand back and let the process happen without interfering. This is why a retreat, which is just a place to do nothing intelligently, can have such excellent results.

Why Are Our Minds So Chaotic?

A truly healthy mind can go into states of extraordinary beauty as well as functioning very nicely during the day. It is a recipe for a long and happy life. Unfortunately, we can't make the mind healthy just by wishing it. We have to clear out the garbage first, and most of us would rather do anything but that.

Why is there so much rubbish in our minds? Why do we feel so stressed and confused much of the time? It's easy to blame our hectic modern lives, our miserable jobs or our lack of the things we think we need for happiness, but all of this is secondary. It's not what happens to us that matters. It's how we react to it.

Some people can be serene and joyful in a concentration camp. Others are paralyzed by anxiety in the midst of trouble-free lives. Whether we live in heaven or hell depends largely on our response to what happens to us.

Living is often painful. We all carry wounds—big, small and invisible—and are hurt, to some degree, almost every day. If we accept the inevitable pains and disappointments without getting unduly upset by them, we are psychologically healthy.

But if we react badly to what life offers, we squirm like a worm on a hook, trapped by chronic fear, anger or desire. These choked emotions permeate the mind and slowly poison us over the years. The mind runs around in fruitless circles, and the body ages rapidly under the strain.

Compromising Our Emotional Expression

Hardly any of us act with the emotional freedom of a two-year-old. To be civilized human beings, we often have to repress our emotions, play it cool when we feel hot and pretend to things we don't feel. We also need the shock response, which enables us to go emotionally numb to cope with a crisis.

We all need to be able to put feelings on hold until we can release them safely. Unfortunately, we often don't release them at all. We prefer to appear cool, capable and always in control. We lock our messy feelings in the basement and try to forget about them.

Unfortunately we can only postpone their expression. The emotions won't go away and die. They wait in the basement with a lifetime's worth of other buried feelings for any chance to emerge. They continually seep back into consciousness as unwanted moods or psychosomatic pains. We feel bad without knowing why.

Emotions are very physical things. The word "e-motion" literally means "to move out." Feelings want to move from the core of our body either upward, as in the case of anger or joy, or downward, as in the case of fear or sorrow.

If we don't block our feelings, they move through easily and equilibrium returns. We see this pattern of tension and release occur very quickly in little children. It is, however, like a storm or a fever. It incapacitates us while it's happening. A person giving way to grief, anger or desire is temporarily uncivilized. He or she is unable to go to work or get the kids off to school.

Most full expressions of emotion will not be tolerated by the people around you. (Rightly so, I might add, since most strong emotion is blind.) It may satisfy your body to vent your rage, but the social consequences can be catastrophic. So you freeze your emotion or leak it out in small doses over days. Unfortunately, the deep freeze eventually overloads and breaks down, usually in your middle years.

I once analyzed a dream in which exactly this image arose. A woman dreamed that her refrigerator had broken down. When she looked in the freezer, she found the dismembered corpse of her estranged husband. It was starting to thaw. She would have to take each piece out with her hands to dispose of it.

She realized that this related to the way she "froze up" years earlier. She left her husband because she couldn't cope with his wasting sickness, and she felt bad about this. She also thought this might be the cause of her recurring skin cancers. It was now seven years later and she was emotionally stronger. It was time to take out the corpse of those frozen feelings and let it thaw.

Awareness Is the Best Therapy

It is a psychological axiom that a patient has to become aware of his trauma to be healed. A therapist rarely "gets rid of" a patient's childhood trauma, for example. She just enables the client to see it with clarity and detachment. For some reason, and it's still not clear why, this awareness alone does the trick.

Meditation operates the same way. As you sit in silence, your subtle discontent and confusion inevitably come to the surface. Whether you realize it or not, you are learning to watch it with increasing calm and detachment.

It starts with the distractions. Every meditator knows that when you try to focus, you're likely to get distracted. You find yourself thinking about work or food or money or last night's TV. Your body feels tired and sore and you don't like the scratchy mood you're in. You feel all these "distractions" are undermining your meditation.

In fact, you could say, like Shakespeare, "Sweet are the uses of adversity that feelingly persuade me who I am." This mental clutter is who you are in this moment. It won't go away unless you acknowledge it. As soon as you can "just watch" it dispassionately, the healing begins.

I particularly notice this in my evening classes. Someone bustles into the room, hyped up and cheerful. Five minutes into the meditation, she realizes she's actually quite exhausted and irritable. Though she resents her chaotic mind, as she recognizes and ticks off the thoughts, they somehow get sorted out. After fifteen minutes she feels more in touch with herself and settled. In a single meditation she goes from chaos to some degree of clarity.

Layers of Discontent

Initially you have to detach from the distractions. Once you relax, you're in a detached state anyway and you can watch your thoughts and feelings with relative clarity. Gradually you can see the deeper layers of feeling and memory within you. As you "just watch" them, they lose their grip on you. The little traumas need to be noticed before you're free of them.

Typically, the immediate problems arise first. Your body feels exhausted and vaguely unwell. Your thoughts are buzzing around unfinished business at work or home. You realize you're not coping very well emotionally. Of course, you also have lovely times as you meditate, but the gritty bits inevitably come through as well.

On retreat, the deeper layers of discontent are likely to emerge fairly soon. You may resist them at first. When you finally face them, it's rather like a boil surfacing on the skin and bursting. It can happen quite fast. You may get two or three periods of resistance and release in a single day. On retreat, it's easier to face the pain you would normally suppress.

Typically, the big traumas of the past, such as a marriage failure or the death of a relative, come through in hundreds of bite-sized pieces. The mind is very kind. It waits till you're calm and feeds you only what you can handle. Instead of one big breakthrough, you get hundreds of small cathartic episodes that can pass in seconds.

It's subtle but very deep and thorough. It covers exactly the same ground as any good therapy but more quietly. A therapist provides a safe container and "adult" perspective to help a client face painful things without repression. Meditation provides the same support by laying a strong base of calm and clarity.

When you're calm, you're not burning much energy. The fires are low. This means that when a feeling of sadness or anger arises, there's not much agitation in the body to fuel it. As the habitual stories around it start up, you can stay cool and see them for what they are— just stories.

This is why there's such an emphasis on tranquility in meditation. When you feel good and in control, you don't need to suppress sadness and anger the way you normally do. You can relax into them and let them move through. You stop being afraid of your own emotions.

The more calm and clear the mind is, the faster the process works. Once you understand the process, it's quite awesome. Whenever the mind is strong and spacious, it will throw out more of the inner toxins, just as the body does when it's fasting.

Toxins Emerging as Physical Sensations

Often when you meditate, you strike resistance. The mind squirms, trying to avoid or get rid of some discomforting thought or feeling. If you assume meditation is only about feeling good, you may think you're not doing it right and stop. This is a mistake. The meditation is actually bearing fruit.

Toxic material can emerge in three obvious ways: as body sensation, as pure feeling or as imagery. Physically you may feel discomfort, itchiness, nausea, muscle tremors, shooting pains, flushes, bloating, agitation and so on. These are typically quite faint but uncomfortable nonetheless. Something feels vaguely wrong inside, though you can't put your finger on it.

You'll eventually realize that a sensation triggered by buried emotion feels different from a purely "physical" sensation. It is more like an intense memory reverberating through the body. Unlike a backache caused by bad posture, for example, it can come and go in a flash. Nonetheless, facing it can be quite a challenge.

One student told me of painful tightness in her upper arms when she meditated. I suggested that it might be a physical memory emerging. A few days later she got the pictures. When she was a child, her mother used to rebuke her by grabbing her by the forearms and shaking her violently. From that moment on, the sensations vanished.

On another occasion a woman said she kept getting images of spots of blood on bathroom tiles. Eventually she remembered what it was about. When she was nine she found her mother dead in the bath—she had slit her wrists. As a child, my student had coped as you naturally would, by repressing much of her reaction. With the maturity of an adult, she was able to let it surface.

Most buried emotions emerge just as emotion without accompanying pictures. Some are obviously anger, resentment, despair or fear, but many are just the queasy, off-color, awkward, indefinable moods that seem to come and go without any reason. Whatever is happening, the basic instructions don't change: just watch it all with detachment.

In time we get to know ourselves and our body/mind rhythms very well. This can be quite a revelation. We are often not at all who we thought we were, or who we are supposed to be. We may notice emotions, images and thoughts that are completely unlike our usual sense of self.

The Swiss psychologist Jung called this "integrating the shadow," though more often it's an acknowledgment of conflicting inner voices and feelings. Strange as all this can be, it's grounding and illuminating to recognize it. No wonder our psyche is rather turbulent at times! No wonder we can't dominate it all with our conscious mind.

Bliss and Trance

As the mind lets go of its hidden tensions, it becomes easier to focus and enter deep states of absorption. Once you leave all sense of self behind, what remains is pure consciousness. In this state, you barely know who or what you are.

Yet it's utterly radiant and blissful. It can be profoundly tranquil or rich in visionary images. In this state, unhealthy emotions vanish utterly, like snowflakes in a fire. With no self to defend, all fear and anger disappear. It is so lovely that all desire and craving for other things evaporate. No aversion or attraction, conscious or unconscious, can get a foothold. All that remains is effortless love and acceptance.

Paradoxically, absorption happens only when "you" stop trying to achieve it. If you want something, both "you" and the desire are in the mind, so absorption can't arise. "Don't try to awaken," as they say in Zen. "Just sit." You drop into absorption when the last of the subtle attractions and aversions vanishes.

Once you drop into the object, a strange thing can happen. The object vanishes also. There is simply infinite space and bliss. Originally, you were one with the object. Now you are one with nothing. You are like a cat at a mouse hole, intensely alert. But even the cat has gone. This is the first stage of trance.

You have merged into the background vibration of pure consciousness itself. Actually, it is always there, like the background hum of the Big Bang resonating through the universe.

In this state, the mind becomes unified. The psychic energy, usually scattered into a thousand thoughts, now streams up and down the spinal column. This can be felt as an almost liquid light. It is described as the nectar of the gods, or like "sugar cane juice," melting the bound energies in the central channel.

When the mind unifies, nothing is excluded. You feel one with God, nature and all humanity—including those you hate! You are no longer at war with yourself or anyone or anything. Even your suffering is perfect in its own way. Nothing is lacking. What more could you possibly want?

Of course, it would be nice to stay in that state longer than we do. It rarely lasts more than a few seconds or minutes, but its aftereffects can be enormous. It is an extremely healthy and life-giving state. This is when cancers may start to dissolve or the buried grief and anger of decades may disintegrate. This is our first glimpse of paradise and, according to the great mystics, the only place we will ever find it.

Everyday Emotional Health

In absorption, you fall in love with the object and forget everything else. The feeling then flows back into ordinary consciousness and becomes another kind of love. We're now able to face everything that enters our minds and lives with an open heart. We accept every thought, feeling, sensation, human being, plant, animal and situation just as it is, without wishing it otherwise. We grow toward a love that has no limits.

Occasionally we meet people like this. Walt Whitman's biographer said it took him years to realize that Whitman never felt animosity toward anyone. He wasn't pretending to be nice. He actually loved and appreciated every human being he ever met.

We often wish we could trash our horrible thoughts and feelings and keep only the good ones. We would prefer to landscape our mental jungle and turn it into an Italian Renaissance garden. Unfortunately, fighting against the jungle inevitably fails.

In meditation, we give a little space to our unwanted thoughts and feelings. We give them their minute on stage. We don't have to act on them, but they're definitely part of us and of other people and of life itself. Though it's hard to admit that they're all there and maybe that they even have a right to be there, this acceptance is the only thing that works in the long run.

The Many Flavors of Meditation

People often say to me, "I've been meditating for months but I don't know if I've reached it yet." So is meditation an ideal state you strive to attain, or is it a variety of states sharing common traits? Beginners typically believe the first, while skilled meditators know it is the second. In this chapter, I'll explain the many flavors of meditation.

People also say, "I'm not sure if I'm doing it right." They usually assume that meditation is a state of blissful tranquility with an empty mind, and this rarely happens for them. If you regard entry into paradise as a sign of a correct meditation, you are bound to feel a failure most of the time. It's not a good ideal. However, there are sensible ways to evaluate any meditation, and I'll explain these later in the chapter.

The "Perfect" Meditation

Sometimes you go into a beautiful state and you know, "That's it! That's what I want! This is real meditation. Now I know how to do it." The Buddhists would say, "Tut, tut. If you want something badly, it's bound to make you miserable." And, damn it all, they're right! For the next ten meditations you struggle to get back there—and fail.

This "perfect" state will appear often enough if your skills are adequate. It also depends on factors beyond your control, such as the kind of day you've had and the mood you were in before you started.

Nonetheless, you get glimpses of it in most meditations. It's when those fleeting seconds become continuous for half a minute or a minute that it starts to feel "perfect."

So what is it like? It is a blissful tranquility. It is tranquil because the body becomes very still as it goes into stage one (or "borderline") sleep. It's blissful because you're still awake enough to enjoy it, yet you've left behind your waking concerns and sense of self.

In contrast with the densely packed thoughts of waking life, the mind feels vast and empty. Nonetheless, there can be a delicate effervescence of images and embryonic thoughts behind the emptiness. This background hum of life gives the emptiness a blissful quality rather than a dead one. If you can stabilize the mind here, it becomes the first of the "samadhi" or trance states.

Typically, you slip in and out of this samadhi state fairly rapidly. You touch it for a few seconds, then you're just out of it. It's almost as good being in its vicinity, suffused by the memory of it. Most people are very happy to be in the pre-samadhi state.

As soon as a beginner has moments of clear wakefulness in stage one sleep, she'll taste this state. The only difference between her and more skilled meditators is that they can string more seconds together before slipping out of it.

Even this state comes with variations. When you lose it, you commonly slip down a notch into unconsciousness. If you're good at this, you don't fall off the chair, but the mind really has gone blank.

With skill this can be a more profound state of meditation, but much more commonly it's just a state of controlled sleep. People come out of it saying, "I don't know where I was the last few minutes," and they're usually quite pleased with themselves. Monks or people who go on long retreats often use this state to recuperate and usually need less sleep at night as a result.

The Typical Meditation—Beta to Alpha to Theta

A typical meditation goes through three stages: tense, relaxing and relaxed. As you go through these stages, your brainwaves literally slow down. The fast waves are called beta, the slower ones are called alpha and theta. You produce beta when you're tense, alpha when you're relaxing and theta when you're relaxed.

When in beta, you're actively chasing thoughts. In alpha, the mind is more oriented to the senses and inclined to wander. In theta, you are on the borderline of sleep, with a sense of space, abandonment of self, and occasional dream imagery.

Strange to say, the most useful state is the pre-samadhi, or alpha, state, in which you are focused but still aware of background thoughts and sensations. Most of your meditation time will be spent here, learning to detach from thoughts and watch them from a distance. This is where you do the spade work and get the mind clean. Since you don't know what's in there until you look it can take a long time.

If you've had a shocking day and the mind is wild, your meditation will feel messy and rather unsatisfying. Yet the messiest meditations are often the most productive. When you disconnect from the worst garbage, you can relax quite rapidly. You may not feel happy, and you won't go into samadhi, but you'll be in a much healthier state afterward. If you're really agitated, you may not even approach theta, yet just the shift from beta to alpha would make this a "good" meditation.

Collapsing into Sleep—Beta to Theta

Some people virtually bypass the alpha state. They collapse into sleep within a minute of sitting down. It's not very elegant, and it probably indicates a manic lifestyle, but it's exactly what they need. They're exhausted and probably suffering sleep deprivation as well. Most of us don't get enough sleep, but these people often suffer additionally from sleep apnea or jumpy legs syndrome that keep waking them at night. They benefit most from very short, but frequent, meditations during the day.

I usually do two or three meditations in a class. I find that many people are sleepy in the first (I don't let them actually go to sleep) and more awake in the second and third. You can also get this cycle in a single meditation. After two or three minutes, you may collapse into a virtual sleep state where you just can't focus at all. After ten or twelve minutes, however, the body and mind have recuperated somewhat and you get the right balance: relaxed body and alert mind.

Thinking While You Meditate

If you meditate once a day or less, you'll tend to think of meditation as a relaxed and often sleepy state. That's usually what you need and what you get. But if you sit more often than this, you'll have many sessions where the mind is clear and in control throughout.

These bright meditations allow you to see in great detail how your waking mind works. You pick up the subtle attractions and aversions and notice the subliminal commentaries and judgments and their consequences.

When the mind is emotionally clear, you can even return to thinking, but of a very different kind. It's more like watching the mind think. It does the work for you. It's a kind of lateral, quick-firing thought that is aware of your feelings but not driven by them. Ideally, you control it very lightly, but you can stop it when it's getting stuck and redirect it. It has an effortless and playful quality.

The key to this kind of thinking is keeping the body deeply relaxed. You know you're losing it when you feel the body tightening. If you relax right down to the sleep threshold, the quality of thought gets even finer. In particular, the mind thinks in images rather than words.

People often do little bursts of thinking in a meditation. Of course this apparently goes against the rules, but it's so useful they can't help themselves. When you relax, you often see a problem from a different angle. "Of course! That's the answer," you think, and you process it a little so you don't lose it.

Even the best of meditators will do some thinking when they meditate. No one goes on a three-month retreat just to become tranquil. They also want to sort a few things out while they're there. They use the undisturbed tranquility to think better. I suspect many of them do a lot of thinking.

Most thinking undermines our mental clarity and relaxation. It spends the capital we're accumulating, yet we all do it. This is often why we learn to meditate in the first place: to be able to think more clearly.

There is no point in demonizing our tendency to think while we meditate. We just have to do it moderately. First, I recommend you at least acknowledge to yourself when you're thinking. Since it often takes place quietly in the background, you can pretend that it's not happening or that it doesn't matter.

Second, when you think on a subject, spend as little time as possible on it. Just spend a few sentences on it. Don't try to finish it off. Be willing to let it go rapidly. It's much better to quickly process something than semiconsciously chew over it for several minutes.

Third, remain in touch with the breath or the body. If you're half with the thinking and half with the body, you won't get swept away so easily. Check the body every ten seconds or so for signs of rising tension.

Fourth, relax before you start actively thinking. If you try to process thoughts while you're tense, you won't relax, and your thinking won't be very productive. The quality of thought improves exponentially the deeper you relax. Thinking while in theta can be very inspired.

Miserable Meditations

If you are ill, in pain, distressed, on medication or your life is in turmoil, your meditation will highlight that. It will give you more balance and perspective and relax your body, but it won't work as a happy pill or a pain-killer.

Unpleasant meditations do invaluable work. If you can face up to your pain and distress without running away, you rob it of its power over you. Acknowledging a bad headache is the first stage in releasing it. Recognizing that you are miserable is much healthier than pretending you're okay.

Even the best of meditators will have chaotic sessions at times. Much of this is shadow stuff coming to the surface. Good meditators are often rather controlling types. They enjoy the serenity of "just watching" and are shocked when the disobedient, impulsive side of their psyche emerges.

Which Meditation Is the Best?

All these meditations have different brainwave profiles. The "perfect" meditation state—lucid theta—is usually just an occasional few seconds or a minute at most. It's often mixed with delta, producing a blissful but barely conscious unconsciousness. It also comes in combination with alpha and even beta when emotion-free thinking takes place.

A typical meditation has a beta-alpha-theta profile, and it may take a good ten or fifteen minutes until you feel you've arrived. Most formal sittings will be like this.

If you're exhausted, you leap straight from beta to theta: asleep in a minute. If you're very agitated or, conversely, not tired at all, you may stay in alpha and never cross the theta threshold.

All the meditations I've described have a positive outcome, despite their differences. Don't be fooled into thinking that theta is best just because it's so pleasant. In reality theta is just the fruit of all the spade work and hard labor that takes place in alpha. And alpha can be sustained indefinitely through the day, whereas theta cannot.

While you try to steer the meditation as best you can, the outcome largely depends on factors beyond your control: how stressed or relaxed or exhausted you are to start with; your state of health and the kind of day you've had; the amount of available time you've got; how long since your last meditation; what your intentions are and so on.

Personally, I just do my best when I meditate and accept what turns up. It's invariably a mirror to my state of mind and health at that moment. It can be deep or shallow or wild or serene or bizarre or humdrum. Personally, I like this uncertainty. I'm glad my mind is so mercurial. I am quite happy to sit down and "just watch" what happens.

Although I do have goals when I meditate, the biggest is self-acceptance. It's not that easy to say "yes" to my passing moods and sensations, but it's very satisfying when I can. In contrast, I'm quite suspicious of my efforts at self-improvement. I find this invariably involves tension, resistance, aversion and longing to some degree. It seems to lack the necessary ingredients for a good outcome.

"Am I Really Meditating?"

You can't answer this question unless you know what you're trying to do. If you're striving for the perfection of the lucid theta state, then the answer will often be "no." You're bound to fail most of the time. If, however, you're trying to relax the body and get the mind clearer, the situation is quite different.

The best way to check your meditation is to ask, "Am I more relaxed and is my mind clearer than when I started?" There should be no mystery about this. If you've trained yourself to recognize the physical signs of relaxation, you can assess it objectively.

Similarly, it shouldn't be hard to assess whether the mind is clearer. It's unlikely to be blank, but it's probably moving more slowly and deliberately. You can direct it more easily, and the thoughts have a lower emotional charge behind them. This is a clearer and more workable mind.

You can also ask yourself during the sitting, "Am I meditating right now?" You could ask an even simpler question: "Am I focused?" If you've lost your meditation object, you'd have to wonder. I'd suggest that you're meditating only when you're consciously focused or consciously watching with detachment.

On the other hand, if you're sitting in a pleasant dreamy state, you're just relaxing. This is not an unhealthy state, but it's not meditating. People often space out, daydream and fall asleep when they "meditate." They can get defensive about this, saying, "Isn't this what meditation is about? Being relaxed?"

Meditation is invariably described as a relaxed and *alert* state. It's only when you're consciously focused or watching thoughts that you detach from them. You have to be alert to get the mind clear.

Meditation implies relaxation, but relaxation doesn't imply meditation. Any time you sit, you'll actually alternate between these two. In the moments when you're consciously focused and watching, you're meditating. When you're losing it a bit and drifting away, you're just relaxed.

Is this important anyway? If you check, you'll find it's only the moments you're actually meditating that do the work. That's the engine. When you're just relaxing, you're dissipating the results. Only when you're focusing and watching is the body relaxing and the mind becoming clearer.

If you did a sitting where you were meditating 50 percent of the time and just relaxing the other 50 percent, that would be a good sitting. Occasionally you have a stunning session where you crank it up to a 90-percent-to-10-percent ratio. If the ratio shifts the other way and you just sit in a daze of dreamy thoughts, you're likely to give up meditating pretty soon. It'll be unsatisfying and finally not worth the time.

The most time-efficient meditations are the short ones. It's easy to be totally with it for most of a two-minute meditation. But if you sit for an hour, the average quality could be very poor. In fact a good fifteen-minute sitting can have as much actual meditation in it as an undisciplined hour-long sitting.

Years of training has made me appreciate the benefits of discipline. Even in the deepest states, I try to hold my focus, though I frequently change it as well. And I always aim for the highest quality of dispassionate awareness and check how it fluctuates. Sometimes I check the quality several times a minute. In those times when my mind is vague, I just do the best I can without criticizing myself. If I'm clear, I enjoy it without getting attached to it.

Why Meditation May Fail to Work

Meditation is a relatively simple and clear skill. Unfortunately, many people get mediocre results with it. I have seen many long-time meditators who are not happy or well-balanced people.

First, meditating just to relax will always have limited value. People who feel that meditation should be a letting go of all effort will miss the point. It takes a little discipline to cut loose from the thoughts that make you tense. If you think of meditation as a kind of day-dreaming or oblivion, you'll waste a lot of time. Unfortunately, people do use meditation for just this purpose, as a kind of organic sedative.

People understand about focusing, but many don't know about dispassionately watching the thoughts go by. It's like trying to fly with one wing. They are forever trying to block out thoughts and failing unless all the conditions are right. Focusing alone works only if you've got something big to tune into, such as group chanting or a physical activity.

For the same reason, many people can only meditate in the special atmosphere of religious or personal development groups, with some-one leading them by the hand. This is meditation as a kind of volun-tary hypnosis. But once you walk out the door or stop chanting, you can no longer meditate. It's a place-specific experience, not a portable skill.

Even experienced meditators can fail to understand the basic skills. They can count the breaths for hours, but they're not really focused on them. They are relaxed but lost in an endless stream of quiet thinking.

The results of regularly sitting like this can be worse than no meditation at all. You may be giving yourself an hour a day to do noth-ing but think. It's not surprising that many meditators are addicted to introspection and somewhat dissociated from the physical world.

Meditation is basically a self-therapy, and therapies work best with a specialist to reality-check you and puncture your self-deceptions. In theory, a meditation teacher should do this. In reality, it almost never happens. The students don't report, and the teacher is too busy to ask.

Meditation teachers usually act as instructors or as spiritual leaders, but not as therapists. They don't tune into you personally as a counselor would. They may not even know your name, but they will tell you what to do.

Most Western teachers have incomplete training or none at all apart from their own experience. Many have just attended a few retreats or workshops and taken it from there. They often teach just one technique to everyone.

In contrast, a Burmese teacher was expected to have ten years training before he started to teach. He learned a range of practices for different situations and personality types. It also takes a long time to understand the trickiness of the mind. Unfortunately, Asian teachers usually lack what we would regard as good teaching skills: they generally preach or lecture instead.

Meditation Plus

The Buddha was of the opinion that meditation was all you needed. You don't need religious or philosophic beliefs, a teacher or a tradition, supportive friends or a good education. You don't even need him! It's all incidental if your eye is clear. A calm, clear and self-reflective mind is a superb foundation for anything you do.

However, meditation itself is so simple and versatile that it blends easily with many activities. Just as water is the basic ingredient of whisky, fruit juice, herbal teas and sport drinks, so meditation mixes with many other disciplines and is often confused with them.

Like water, a calm clear mind doesn't have a strong flavor. It invariably takes its flavor from the setting or the teacher or the philosophy in which you meet it. These can be so emotionally charged they can overwhelm the meditation component within them.

If you're meditating for spiritual purposes or to visualize your future or to fill your body with healing energy, you may forget to relax the body adequately or get the mind clear first. If you don't develop these basic skills, then your meditative results will be patchy no matter how important your aspirations are.

I usually describe myself as a technical teacher. I teach my students how to drive. It's up to them where they want to go. Unfortunately, if they're too preoccupied with their goals to learn to drive well, it won't help them much. It's good to remember that meditation as a skill is actually distinct from the many purposes it's used for. Sometimes it fits well, and sometimes it doesn't. We'll now look at some of those purposes.

Relieving Stress and Anxiety

Meditation is a natural stress reliever. If you don't relax adequately, you feel habitually tense. If this continues over months and years, the physical discomfort alone can push you into chronic anxiety. The next stage is to have panic attacks where you feel you can't cope with the simplest things (which is true). If you don't reverse things here, you're heading for a nervous breakdown or serious illness.

In a recent class, I had three state managers from different firms. When I asked why they wanted to learn meditation, the first said, "I can barely cope any longer." The second said, "I had a heart attack at thirty-eight." The third said, "I had a nervous breakdown seven months ago."

Meditation, the art of relaxing consciously, is the perfect antidote for extreme stress, though lifestyle changes may also be necessary. Minute for minute, I doubt if any other stress management strategy works as well as meditation. I find that high achievers, being naturally diligent, learn the skill quite rapidly.

Meditation also works well for performance anxiety. Musicians, sports people, students and anyone who has to put on a performance at work need to monitor their tension/relaxation levels well. I've helped several musicians and sports people achieve their best with the help of meditation.

For example, one young singer told me that her tension levels would peak too early, so she'd be tired by the time she went on stage. I helped her prepare for a national competition—which she won, leading to an international career.

Meditating for a Better Quality of Life

Stress and ill health can make you look at your quality of life. If you're too young to retire, at least you can take time to smell the roses.

Meditation, by enhancing the sensual function and bringing you into the moment, makes you do just this.

For many people, "meditation" is less a formal practice than a reminder to slow down, relax and enjoy what they are doing. They try to integrate the qualities of awareness and be present in all they do.

I find that older people who learn to detach from a lifetime of worry often become passionate about some new activity or study. It becomes their meditation, relaxing and inspiring them. Whether it's a sport, a study or an art, it has the same quality of internal satisfaction as meditation, rather than the external rewards of money or status.

Meditating with Yoga, Tai Chi and Martial Arts

Any sport can become a meditation if you consciously pay attention to what you're doing. Traditionally, yoga, tai chi and the martial arts have deep connections with meditation and may well be the first place you encounter it.

Yoga, in particular, by stretching the muscles is the exact antidote to tension, which of course contracts them. Yoga trains you in very precise body awareness, which is a huge advantage when you meditate. I've done yoga on and off for thirty years and usually do two or three hours a day if I'm on retreat.

Of course there is more to yoga than stretching. This is where the overlaps between meditation and other disciplines get confusing. While yoga often has an explicit meditation component, it can also be a lifestyle discipline including diet and other matters, and it can involve philosophical and religious beliefs.

Hope, Belief and Meditation

In our consumer culture gone mad, many groups clamor for our bodies, souls and/or money. Meditation is frequently found in combination with inspirational ideas, hopes and beliefs. This is a huge business. Hope is a very saleable commodity.

Sometimes our hopes are satisfied by adopting a religious path. Much more commonly, we buy or do or attend things in the hope or belief that we'll benefit. We can't check the hard facts about whether they work or not, because they're usually unverifiable anyway. Testimonials and advertising take the place of evidence.

Belief and hope can be good for your health. Research has shown that people who have something to believe in are commonly happier than people who don't. However, this has nothing to do with the veracity of the beliefs. Believing itself relieves stress.

Many of us think and worry far too much. Belief and hope, however, undermine the habit of analytical thought. They bring order and a road map to a chaotic world and therefore relieve anxiety. Belief and hope, in other words, have the same physiological effects as meditation: they help you relax and feels good. And they can be addictive.

Meditation, belief and hope are frequently found together. When you meditate at a church, monastery, New Age gathering or self-development course, how much are you relaxing because of the meditation and how much because of the inspiring ideas?

This mixture of meditation and hope is often a mismatch. At bottom, meditation works differently. It is profoundly empirical, putting you face to face with the raw data of your own feelings and sensations in the moment. It gives you a deep sense of your own truth and individuality that is largely beyond concepts.

Systems that involve hope and belief, however, often involve a flight into fantasy and possibilities. By definition, they can't be tested. The thought involved tends to be rationalizing rather than rational, working toward predetermined conclusions.

I suspect that belief systems benefit from incorporating meditation, but not vice versa. If meditating is part of your religious practice or self-development program, you are likely to understand the ideas in more depth. However, your basic meditative qualities of calm detachment and clarity of mind may not improve at all and may even decline.

Cults Are Not What They Seem

If you learn meditation in a Christian or Buddhist or Hindu setting, you know there's a religious aspect to it. It's aboveboard. You know what the deal is. This is what distinguishes a religion from a cult.

Cults, however, are masters of deception. The vast majority don't look like cults at all. Like the Mafia, they operate behind false fronts. Most are not religious at all. They just exploit your spiritual hunger or emotional confusion to get at your money.

Cults operate on deceptive advertising. Some are obviously cultist or way-out, but they can present themselves as fitness classes, self-development courses, study groups, educational institutes, weight-loss programs or staff management regimes. Anything that offers you a new and inspiring belief to improve your life could be a cult. At some point you realize you've spend a lot of money and time and gotten nothing.

It's good to realize that meditation and yoga are frequently used as bait. Many famous yoga schools are religious groups that run yoga classes to recruit members. The biggest challenge for any religion or cult, or for that matter anyone trying to make money, is, "How do you get people in the door?" Once they're in and you've got them feeling relaxed and good about themselves, the rest is easy.

Meditation Often Leads to Dependency

Cults and lifestyle businesses frequently use meditation and similar devices to put people into hypnotic and obedient states. It can happen very easily. If you talk at an audience for an hour, about half will be in a light hypnotic state by the end. They'll be relaxed, because they're doing nothing. Their critical faculties will largely be cut off by the speaker's words. And they'll be prone to suggestion. They'll find what the speaker says to be plausible.

Religions and cults can be very good at inducing this relaxed, suggestible state. In Indian gatherings, you typically sing songs before the guru speaks. Many churches do the same. Any kind of body movement like yoga or tai chi will also get you out of your head. A leader speaking in an incantatory way or guiding a meditation works perfectly. People love it and keep coming back for more.

Even if you just attend a group in someone's home, the meditation you do there can induce dependency. It's a relaxed, uncritical, nonverbal state that feels good. In a group setting, it's often hypnotically induced by subtle directions, past associations and nonverbal hints. And guided meditations are often designed to suggestively reshape the way you think.

Even the smallest and most benign group has its unspoken direction and values. If you're dependent on the group to meditate at all, you may feel obliged or be persuaded to take them on board.

Though meditation in its essence is as bland as water, it always takes on a flavor from the way you encounter it. In time, however, you should find your own flavor. It should taste of you. If you don't know how to find and sustain this inner taste, you're likely to stay with the flavor of the group.

Of course, the group ideology may be exactly what you want. You will be meditating, but it is meditation plus. You can combine it with spiritual healing, mind-power training, Tibetan Buddhism, restructuring your thought patterns, developing your financial skills, doing compassionate work or making the chi flow. Just remember that meditation, the art of relaxing the body and clearing the mind, is not exactly the same as any of these.

Self-development

Meditation has close links with the great traditions of self-development toward the perfection of the mind. In Burma, monks were expected to go through a sequence of verifiable experiences over the years. Tibetans would commit themselves to lifetimes perfecting the virtues essential for awakening.

A Tibetan professor, rather like a Catholic priest, was expected to contemplate the doctrine for decades, until he was utterly convinced of its truth and could convincingly argue it with others. Christian, Islam, Judaic, and shamanic traditions, as well as countless smaller mystery cults, map out stages in the development of the perfect human being.

Common to most of these are intense self-analysis, acknowledgment of one's shortcomings and an image of perfection that you strive to achieve.

In all these systems it is hard to distinguish meditation as a healthy and natural path of inner growth from forms of self-indoctrination. There is no doubt that despite their great antiquity, they utterly fail many people who enter them. There are miserable and defeated priests and monks the world over.

The same is probably true of modern self-development regimens that are not overtly religious. Freudian psychoanalysis, for example, is based on unverifiable or false hypotheses and demands submission to the superior wisdom of the analyst (disagreement is called "resistance"). It also promises the earth, costs a fortune and works very poorly as a therapy, as many studies have shown.

Nonetheless, its enormous financial success has inspired many imitators. New therapies and self-development regimes appear every year, each with its own extravagant claims and unverifiable premises. When such systems are criticized for their indifferent results, they fall back on excuses that have been used for centuries.

They argue that the obstacles to growth are so huge that you can't expect an easy solution, or that you're going through a healing crisis and will eventually break through, or that your negativity or pride or false views make you resistant to the truth or simply that you need to try harder.

This may seem like a terrible heresy, but I think it is good to sometimes question the whole idea of self-development. Is it just an attempt to be someone other than who we are? Is the idea that we can constantly get better and better just a myth without foundation? There is plenty of evidence that things change, but is improvement only in the eye of the beholder? Is this just another neo-Darwinian assumption that everything is evolving toward perfection and we just have to find the right way for us? I don't know the answer to this, but it's worth considering occasionally.

Self-awareness

There are many Western techniques and disciplines that value self-awareness, the ability to look at one's body and mind honestly and dispassionately. This is quite different from analyzing oneself according to a system or trying to attain to an ideal.

Meditation, by enhancing self-awareness, can be excellent with physical disciplines such as yoga or sports where you attune yourself exactly to the reality of your body. It helps with artistic disciplines, where you seek inspiration and examine in detail your perception of the world. It can help with philosophic disciplines in which you ask yourself, "Who am I? What is it to be human?"

Awareness helps greatly in those pragmatic therapies that encourage you to see yourself and your self-deceptions just as they are. These are therapies that give primacy to the client's experience, rather than to ideological constructs. Quite simply, if you see clearly what's causing you pain, you can do something about it. Those who work in the healing arts know quite well how people suffer because of their mental blindness.

It's not surprising that many Western meditation teachers are also counselors or psychologists. Their curiosity about how the mind works probably took them from one to the other. Both meditators and psychologists need a keen eye to look below the surface and to distinguish fantasy from fact. Furthermore, a psychologist who is calm and self-aware is unlikely to project her own emotional issues onto a client.

Finally, meditation helps enormously in the journeying of your "soul," however you understand this mysterious word. By giving access to deeper states of consciousness, you see deeply into your moods, feelings, dreams and intuitions. Though unstable and hard to grasp, they are just as real as your big toe—and possibly more so.

Summary

A calm clear mind is enormously valuable. It de-stresses you rapidly, body and mind. It keeps your body healthy and helps it heal when it's sick. It helps you cope well with dramas and enjoy life more. You learn to focus and study better and let the unnecessary mental clutter go rapidly.

You perform better at work, on stage or on the sports field. You think more clearly, and think laterally and creatively. You tolerate your own shortcomings and those of others more easily.

When meditation combines with disciplines that involve belief or hope, some caution is required. It is frequently used to induce a hypnotic, obedient and uncritical state of mind that makes you vulnerable to manipulation.

Meditation blends perfectly with disciplines, skills and therapies that value self-awareness and have a certain rational curiosity about how the body and/or mind works. It helps you find yourself as an individual.

PART TWO

The Bedrock Practices

The Basic Principles

Meditation is a technique that relaxes the body and clears the mind. So why is it so hard to relax and clear the mind of clutter? The answer is obvious: we think too much.

Thinking is useful, but most of us overdo it. We get exhausted by the endless stream of hopes, worries, fantasies, plans and dialogues. Unfortunately, our thoughts don't stay in the head. They also stir up the body, keeping us tense during the day and unable to relax well at night. A busy mind agitates our heads and our bodies equally.

Usually when we find we're thinking in circles, we try to block out our thoughts or finish them off. But neither option works well, and meditation takes a different tack. Its approach is one of radical simplicity: you just sit still and do nothing. Or "just watch" the inner dialogues without engaging them.

It might sound easy, but have you ever tried it? The mind is very reluctant to do nothing at all. Even a calm mind is naturally exploratory and curious. So in lieu of doing nothing (which is impossible), we do something as simple and stress-free as possible.

To divert ourselves from thought, we focus on something. To keep the mind out of trouble, we pay attention to something simple (like the breath), or something pleasant (such as music). We switch from thinking mode to sensing mode. The mind will often detour back to thinking, but even intermittent focus on a sensual object will relax us. It acts as an anchor, slowing down the restless mind.

While focusing, you are also learning to detach from thoughts. You often find you're caught in them and have to break free from their grip. Then you find you can resist the temptation *before* they grab you. As your body and mind settle down, the mental agitation fades and it becomes easier to "just watch" the thoughts come and go in the background, without needing to process them.

Focus, detachment, a passive awareness—these are the core skills in meditation. They all simplify the mental activity and conserve energy. When we do something simple, the body relaxes and the mind goes "Aaaahhh!" We are reverting to a more elementary state of consciousness—a state of being, rather than doing.

Why Does Thinking Make Us So Tense?

Thinking is exhausting. Nearly a third of the body's energy expenditure each day happens in our heads. Furthermore, the more we think, the worse we think. A tired mind can't follow a train of thought and tends to scatter. It gets lost in trivia and frequently blanks out for seconds or minutes at a time. Sometimes we're just "not here" at all.

Thinking may seem a rational activity, but it's often powered by quite gross emotions. Fear (or "anxiety," to use a more polite term) may be driving your thoughts about work. Anger or irritation may underpin your thoughts about family. Desire may be driving your planning for the weekend. As a rule of thumb, the thoughts with the strongest emotions will dominate the others.

Thinking stirs up the body. It activates the sympathetic branch of the nervous system, whose function is to mobilize the body for action. Thinking sends hormonal signals through the body saying, "Stay on guard! We've got things to do. This is no time to relax." This can happen even though you're just trying to unwind on the bus ride home from work.

When you feel stressed, it is very hard to "just watch" thoughts with detachment. The bodily agitation propels you back into your head, vainly seeking a solution. The best way to disconnect from thinking is to focus on something else: to shift your attention to the sense world.

Shifting from Thinking to Sensing

Most meditation objects are sensual things—the breath, the body, sounds, music, a repeated word or phrase. If you listen carefully to the sounds around, or feel the breath rising and falling, you'll find your thoughts slipping into the background. They rarely disappear entirely, but it's quite enough to turn down the volume on them. Sensing slows us down from the volatility of thought to the immediacy of just feeling, just seeing, just hearing.

Thinking produces "beta" brainwaves, which are fast, erratic and of low amplitude. Sensing produces "alpha" brainwaves which are slower, rhythmic and of high amplitude. You can read this shift on an electroencephalograph after just twenty seconds of sustained sensing. There is nothing fanciful or imaginary about this. Something real is happening in your biochemistry.

Subjectively we feel the shift somewhat differently. Thinking is busy and active, involving concepts of past and future. It is usually powered by some variant of fear, anger or desire. It is a high-energy state, exciting but also exhausting.

Sensing is quite the opposite. It is passive and keeps you in the present. It is emotionally looser, burns less energy and feels more sustainable. It is relaxing and more pleasant.

Being in the Present

We usually spend very little time in the present—probably two or three minutes an hour on average. We live in our minds, and most of that relates to the past and future. We just check into the sense world for a second here and there, so we don't bump into doors or get killed crossing the road.

Since most of our anxieties relate to past and future, we can escape them by entering the present moment. Often we find the world of the senses is a lovely space, full of light and color and beauty that we miss if we are lost in thought. We don't have to live permanently in the present and never think of other things. Just to spend five to ten minutes of each hour on Planet Earth would be a huge improvement.

In fact, we don't need to focus on just one thing to meditate, despite all I've said until now. We just need to be present. We could tune into any sense object at random or move from one to another, and still be detached from thought.

The mind doesn't much like being still, but with a little guidance we can persuade it to stay within boundaries of the sense world. Right now, for example, I can hear the hum of the computer . . . then feel my hand on the wooden desk . . . then hear my chair creak . . . feel my eyes are sore . . . then feel myself swallow . . . I hear a distant car pass.

We notice these incidental sense stimuli quite clearly when we meditate. We don't need to regard them as distractions. They can actually reinforce our sense of being present, and make the meditation more interesting.

For example, while meditating our attention may shift from the breath to the heartbeat to a sound to a slight pain, then back to the breath again, and so on. You could even choose to focus intently on any one of these for a few seconds. Done slowly and deliberately, this still keeps us present and the body relaxes.

Being Relaxed and Alert

People often ask me, "What is the difference between meditation and relaxation?" They correctly suspect that meditation is more than just being half asleep.

Meditation is a calm and alert state of mind. It is when the body is relaxed and the mind is focused. Relaxation, however, is when the mind wanders. It goes from thoughts to feelings to daydreams to sleepiness, and is often vague and out of control. A relaxed state is rarely as still and clear as a good meditation.

Meditation balances relaxation and alertness. Usually we are one or the other—wired up but not relaxed, or relaxed but half-asleep. But with fine-tuning we can achieve the best of both worlds. A meditator can relax deeply and be mentally clear at the same time.

We are most likely to be relaxed and alert when we pay attention to something we enjoy. In other words, something attracts us and we focus on it. We could be:

- listening to music
- watching birds in the backyard
- doing yoga or any exercise deliberately
- having a shower
- eating a peach
- arranging flowers
- lying in bed, listening to wind and rain

Focusing: the First Skill

Focusing is what stops the mind from wandering aimlessly. The basic meditation strategy—focus on something sensual and let the thoughts go—is relatively clear, but it needs practice. Doing something sensual is not the same as focusing on it. We can easily eat a peach without tasting it at all. The mind is very fast and could be anywhere.

Focusing means slowing down and paying attention. When eating a peach, you feel your teeth breaking the skin, the juice on your tongue and saliva flowing. You notice how fresh it is, you savor the mixture of taste and smell, and even hear the sounds of eating. This is good focus: it catches fine detail. It brings the sensations into sharp clarity, like focusing a camera.

Eating one peach like this will give us much more pleasure than gobbling three or four mindlessly. This is how focus works. It draws us in and unifies the mind. Focusing distances us from our habitual thoughts of the past and future.

Some people have trouble with the idea of focus, associating it with knitted brows and grim determination. Some groups even suggest that you shouldn't focus at all but just "let everything go." In meditation, however, focusing is quite gentle. It highlights one thing while still allowing other thoughts and sensations to be in the background.

Focusing occurs naturally when something attracts us—a cloud-scape, a flowering bush, a beautiful body walking by. A child absorbed in a toy is focused, sensing and present. This is a kind of unconscious meditation. The Indian word for focusing—"samadhi"—is a synonym for tranquility and bliss, not effort.

We can't force the mind to focus, but we can gently encourage it. Eventually the mind wants to focus because the results are so satisfying. The mind feels clear, awake and in control, and the body becomes still. This doesn't happen if you just daydream or space out.

Watching with Detachment: the Second Skill

So what happens when you focus, for example, on the breath? You pay attention to it, you feel it rise and fall, you try to catch the end and start of each breath. In other words, you tune into it and try to sense it clearly.

After a few seconds the mind says, "Okay, I've got that. What else shall I do while I'm meditating?" Without telling you, it sneaks off to something else. Soon you realize you've lost the breath and you're thinking about last night's TV.

At this point, you have a choice. You could process that thought the way you normally would, or you could just drop it and return to the breath. If you let it go, you have a moment of liberation. You are detaching from something that is stirring you up, and returning to something simple and stress-free. You might have to do this hundreds of times. It is the spade work of meditating. You can't avoid noticing the thoughts, but you can learn to detach from them quickly.

Even when you are focused well, you'll still notice other thoughts and sensations in the background. If you don't let them distract you from the breath, you are "watching with detachment," or being "passively aware." The thoughts rarely vanish, but you don't have to entertain them. It is said, "You can't stop birds flying overhead, but you can stop them nesting in your hair."

If you have this "witness" or "spectator" perspective you are bound to be peaceful. After all a spectator just watches the show without getting sucked into the dramas. He doesn't have to actually do anything at all.

Focusing and Watching Work Together

Meditating is the art of putting one thing in the foreground while dispassionately noticing other thoughts in the background. These are the two skills in meditation: focusing and "just watching." The first acts like a spotlight, illuminating the object. The second is like a floodlight, picking up peripheral data. Both are essential.

Meditators soon realize they can't fix their mind on a object like putting a pound of butter on a table. Within a few seconds it will attend to the background as well. It goes on a quick border patrol to check what else is happening. The mind is like a wild animal that feeds while periodically lifting its head to look for danger. If done lightly and quickly, this doesn't break the meditation.

This oscillation between foreground and background is natural and necessary. Sometimes it happens a lot and you spend more time out than in. Sometimes it happens very little, and the object holds you easily. But it is impossible to stop. This is just the way the mind works.

Meditators often make themselves miserable by thinking that focusing is "good," and that noticing other thoughts and sensations is "bad." In fact both activities are essential, and you practice both in any meditation. When the mind happens to be focused, you take it deeper. And when the mind is patrolling the borders, then you develop your ability to "just watch" with tolerance and detachment.

In time you may find the dispassionate, clear-seeing mind is even more valuable than the pleasure of focus. Focusing is a temporary

escape from thought, but can't be sustained forever. A clear awareness, however, enables us to look at anything with tolerance and a
certain philosophic humor. Anywhere, anytime, in any situation, you
can reduce your stress by switching into observer mode.

What Happens When You Meditate?

In theory, you could calm the body and clear the mind by focusing on
anything, anywhere while doing any activity. In practice, most people
meditate by sitting in a quiet room, focusing on something obvious
like the sensations of their body. This is a good place to start.

An upright padded chair is best for most Westerners. If you are
very tense, then a reclining chair or lying on the bed will help you relax.
It won't help your clarity of mind, however. You're likely to fall asleep
and lose the meditation. However, you are welcome to do that, if that's
what you want.

So you try to focus on the breath and let other thoughts and sensations pass by. Often the first two or three minutes are quite scrappy.
The unfinished business of the day clamors for your attention as soon
as you sit down. This can be quite annoying but it is necessary and
inevitable. As you notice the little bits and pieces, you partially sort
them out and let them go. This happens almost automatically. It's a
way of checking where you're at.

Gradually it becomes easier to focus. The mind still comes and
goes, but you actually start to feel the breath now. It comes into focus.
You feel the breath rising and falling, and the body expanding and
contracting. You catch the moment of stillness when the breath stops.

By now, you're also picking up more sense data. Sounds often
seem louder and you feel the body starting to relax. Often the limbs
feel heavy and you notice little aches and pains and your latent fatigue
coming to the surface. The out-breath feels loose and soft.

Your brainwaves are shifting from beta (mostly thinking), to alpha
(mostly sensing). Thinking continues but less obsessively. Thoughts
become more random and fragmentary, even dreamlike, and easier to
detach from.

Once you break the grip of thoughts, the body can relax rapidly. If you are at all tired, you soon reach the edge of sleep. This is where theta brainwaves start appearing. You've succeeded in relaxing, but you now have another problem: keeping the mind alert. Usually when the body goes to sleep, the mind follows. To meditate we break that linkage. We aim for a state where the body is asleep but the mind is awake.

Many Westerners tend to associate meditation with a relaxed, daydreamy state at the edge of sleep. They sit in a foggy half-sleep and wonder why they just feel groggy afterward. In fact, they are missing the best part of the meditation.

If you can stay alert at the edge of sleep, the mind detaches from all the remaining thoughts and becomes delightfully clear and still. It feels lucid and spacious. It notices the subtlest sensations with clarity and emotional freedom. It is clear in the sense of "seeing things clearly." Since it straddles the waking and sleep states, it can even look consciously into the dream state.

Meditations commonly go through three stages: tense, relaxing and relaxed. These relate to beta, alpha and theta brainwave patterns. If you can train yourself to stay awake at the edge of sleep, beautiful mind states, deep peace, mental clarity and flashes of insight can occur so often we start to take them for granted.

Yet whether a meditation is pleasant or not, you usually feel better for some time afterward. Even a scruffy meditation can loosen the grip of thoughts and relax the body to some degree. The aftereffects can linger for an hour or two, keeping you more balanced and in touch with yourself. It may have been only five minutes long, but it was five minutes well spent.

Starting with the Breath

To meditate you could focus on any one of a thousand things. Nonetheless, you are also likely to be aware of your body, the sounds around you and your thoughts as well. It happens every time. You may meditate on the breath, for example, but you can't help noticing that your body feels stiff and tired, it's rather noisy outside and you're thinking about money or your girlfriend.

Not surprisingly, these four things—the breath, the body, sounds and thoughts—are also the most common things to meditate on. These are the bedrock practices. There are scores of ways to meditate on the breath or the body. Meditating on random sounds is a simple practice but very useful. And any meditator needs some way of watching thoughts and feelings with clarity.

If we add meditations that use mantra, affirmations, imagery and visual objects we have a very comprehensive range. There is no one practice that suits everyone, but I imagine at least 90 percent of the world's millions of meditators are using some variant of the above. We will explore them all, and a few more besides.

We will start with the breath. It is a very accessible practice. The breath is always with us, and it's easy to focus on. It is often where beginners start, and yet it is a practice with a lot of scope. It matures over time and can last you the rest of your life.

This lesson outlines the instructions for *any* meditation practice by using the breath as a example. When I want to illustrate a point later in this book, I will often use "the breath" to represent "any meditation object." Despite this, you shouldn't assume that focusing on the breath is an integral part of any meditation. It's not. It's just one possible object of focus among many, and it certainly doesn't suit everyone.

Why So Many People Meditate on the Breath

The breath is the number-one favorite practice of people throughout the world. Though some people find it unsuitable, I imagine more people meditate on the breath, in some way, than on all the other practices combined. There are many reasons for this.

The breath is usually a soothing thing to tune into. The gentle ebb and flow of the breath massages the body internally. It is soft, tactile and reassuring. It may evoke memories of our time in the womb, when we were enclosed by our mother's heartbeat and breathing.

The breath tells us exactly how tense or relaxed we are. When tense, the breath feels constricted and held in the chest. As we loosen up, the breath drops through the body. Eventually, it becomes delicate, soft and spacious. We also notice how our thoughts can stir up the breath. It is a perfect mirror to what is happening in our bodies and minds.

The more we relax, the more subtle and evasive the breathing becomes. This forces us to stay alert to keep in touch with it. We also get a taste of stillness and deep space in the gap between the breaths.

The breath mixes well with other objects. It is transparent. We can easily scan the body or say a mantra or watch thoughts or listen to sounds or do a visualization while also meditating on the breath. It also seems to stimulate memory and dream imagery more than other practices.

Meditation: The Breath

These are the basic instructions for any formal meditation. Only sections 3 and 4 specifically relate to the breath. You could focus instead on a mantra, for example, or a body scan or a visualization. You can regard the following instructions as a template for any other formal practice.

1. PREPARATION

Choose a relatively quiet place and give yourself fifteen minutes or more free of interruptions. If it helps, play soft music very quietly in the background. Take a comfortable upright position that allows you to breathe easily. For most people, a straight-backed padded chair is ideal.

2. SHIFT FROM THINKING TO SENSING

Notice the soundscape. Notice how your body feels and let it soften. Take a deep breath or two and sigh gently as you breathe out.

3. FOCUS ON THE BREATH

Go to some place where you can feel the breathing clearly. It could be in the belly or chest or throat or nostrils. When you breathe out, let your mind sink into that place. Feel the breath rise and fall, and the body expand and contract. Don't try to control the breath. Just let it do what it wants to do.

4. COUNT THE BREATHS

To stay on track, count the breaths up to 4, or 8, or 10 repeatedly. You say the word "one" as you breathe out, then "two" on the next out-breath, and so on. Try to keep the count going, even though you're aware of other thoughts and sensations as well.

5. NOTICE THE SIGNS OF THE BODY RELAXING

Your limbs may feel heavy or still or light. You may notice tingling or pulsing on the skin. Aches and pains often become more obvious. And the breath becomes lighter and gentler. Enjoy these feelings.

6. NAME THE DISTRACTIONS

If a thought or sensation persistently distracts you, then try "naming" the content of it: "work," "headache," "chainsaw," "Mary," and so on.

7. EMERGE SLOWLY

Have your eyes open for the last few seconds. Keep the breathing and the face soft. Realize you don't have to speed up just because your eyes are open. Stay passive and enjoy the way you feel. Ask "Am I more relaxed and settled than when I started?"

Let me explain some of these instructions in more detail.

Shift from Thinking to Sensing

This means noticing the body sensations, sounds and sights you normally ignore when you are thinking. Don't worry if some noises irritate you or your body hurts. The stimuli don't have to be pleasant. Sensing alone is enough to slow the mind. The art of "watching with detachment" also means accepting and tolerating things you don't like.

People often feel they have to stay perfectly still to meditate. Relaxing, however, means letting the body go. Good meditators often move slightly from time to time. The face and shoulders soften, the breath becomes looser and little postural adjustments occur. Furthermore, watching these sensations takes you deeper into the present and accelerates the process.

Focus on the Breath

Focusing means "bringing the object into focus," like adjusting a camera lens. This enhances detail, and time slows down. You notice the very moment the breath starts and stops. Focusing is easier if you cultivate an interest in your object. Notice the individuality of each breath.

Don't try to control the breath, or if you are a natural controller, at least control it lightly. This is not the time to do formal breathing exercises. The breath is just a prop to hang the mind on. If we try to breathe deeply and regularly, we may overoxygenate the body, which will make us jumpy. It will also stop the breath slowing down naturally, as it does when we relax.

Because the breath is "transparent," you're likely to notice other thoughts and sensations as well. Focusing means actively highlighting the breath, while passively noticing other things. Remember that the mind naturally oscillates from foreground to background anyway. Don't try to hold the breath in an iron grip. Just rest with it lightly whenever you can.

Counting the Breaths

Because the mind is passive in most meditations, it can get too passive and drift away. There is usually some simple repetitive task at the core of any meditation to keep you on track. In this case we count the breaths.

Counting is easy at first. Then the mind puts the count on automatic pilot and slips away. Counting is a warning device. When you can't remember what the next number is, you know you've lost the breath. And you know exactly what to do next: start counting again.

There are several ways to count. You could just count on the out-breath. Or say "one" on the in-breath, "two" on the out-breath, and so on. Or you could double-count, saying "one" on both the in-breath and out-breath.

People usually count four or eight or ten breaths at a time, and then return to one. Musicians often just "feel" the number they're up to, like sensing a musical phrase. It's quite enough to actually feel the breaths without counting. I once had a class containing five accountants. Counting was not their idea of fun. You could just say "in... out..."

Counting alone is not enough. You still have to consciously feel the breaths or you'll get lost in thought easily. Counting is just a way of pointing you at the breath. And if you're feeling the breath in detail anyway, then counting is redundant.

Naming the Distractions

We always notice background thoughts and sensations when we meditate. If we "just watch" them with detachment, they're not a distraction. Many of them are sensual things anyway. The sounds of traffic or a slamming door, a headache or back pain, a sense of fatigue—all are part of the present moment.

However certain thoughts can become real distractions. You try to let them go, but they hang around and often get more demanding. So what do you do? They usually need to be acknowledged before they let you go. If you want, you can use the technique called "naming the distractions."

If you're distracted, you step back from the thought and consciously identify it. You "name" its content: "Television . . . food . . . work . . . money . . . Susan. . . ." The act of naming is quite different from thinking something through.

Distractions usually grab us from behind. We may have been thinking about Susan unconsciously for minutes before we realized it. By saying "Susan," however, we both acknowledge the thought and stand back from it.

"Naming the distraction" serves to pigeonhole it. The thoughts around Susan don't disappear, but we don't indulge them. They are still in the mind but not center stage. You allow her a place in the mind, but at the periphery. Some people call this "doing the filing."

You could use very general words when you name. You could just say "distraction," or "past" or "future," for example. You could be more precise and name the content of the thought—"Susan"—or the emotion behind it—"sadness." You could even name sensory things that are disturbing you: "garbage truck," "itchy nose," "sore feet."

Not everyone finds that naming works for them. It can make them think more rather than less. Such people find it better to stick with the basic strategy of returning the mind to the breath whenever it roams.

The Biology of Relaxation

People often say to me, "I'm meditating regularly, but I don't know if I'm doing it right." This is a question they should be able to answer. Meditation is a skill, like playing a musical instrument or a sport. If you evaluate what you're doing, you can eliminate errors, improve your abilities and enjoy it much more.

Few people ask the obvious questions:

"What am I trying to do?"

"Am I getting what I want?"

"Can I do this better?," or even,

"Am I relaxing at all?"

Why People Can't Evaluate Their Practice

I have to congratulate anyone who is prepared to sit quietly for a few minutes each day. This will probably do them some good, whatever is going on in their heads. Unfortunately, many meditators fumble around in a fog.

There are reasons for this confusion and lack of clarity. Relaxation is the process that takes us toward sleep, so we progressively lose awareness as we relax. We tend to drift amid thoughts and fantasies. We often "space out" a little and can't even say what we're thinking about. If we fail to stay alert as the body relaxes, it's hard to recognize what's happening.

Meditation is a state of "not-doing," which makes it such a valuable antidote to our busy goal-oriented behavior. It is largely a passive activity, but you can get too passive. Once you realize how exhausted you are and how lovely it is to do nothing, you can get stuck there. Many people sit down at the feet of a guru (or a tradition or practice), and never get going again.

People often meditate poorly because no one can see what they're doing. Anyone can see you hit a bad golf shot, but when you sit perfectly still on your cushion, are you going into advanced states of trance or just worrying about money? Golfers continually give each other tips on playing better, but meditators don't. They rarely discuss their practice or learn from each other.

Finally meditation is hard to talk about because it's largely a non-verbal state anyway. It is a shift from words to sensation, feelings and images, and rational thought seems out of place. If you also see meditation as an esoteric or transcendental experience, you're even less likely to ask, "Is this working?"

Asking the Obvious Questions

Meditation is about relaxing the body and clearing the mind, and these are intimately linked. If the body isn't relaxed, the mind is bound to be restless. Conversely, a still, tranquil body is the foundation for beautiful states of mind.

A useful and important question to ask is, "Am I relaxing?" Meditation involves relaxing the body, quickly and consciously. In this lesson, we'll look at checking your degree of relaxation. We'll talk about clarity of mind later.

Relaxing is not a spiritual mystery. It's a biological process that you can observe easily if you know what to look for. It helps to know what are the signs that tell you you're relaxing, and what degree of relaxation you've reached. If you want to be able to relax quickly and deliberately, it pays to understand this humble process that we usually take for granted.

Relaxation Is Biological

Let us assume you feel tense and anxious after a terrible day at work. As soon as you start to meditate, you feel the body loosening. You have initiated "the relaxation response." Within minutes, every biological system within you is changing from arousal to relaxation.

Once the process is underway, muscle tension will release. Blood pressure will drop and circulation will improve. Breathing will soften and the digestive system will come back to life. Your aches and pains will become more obvious, then gradually fade away. If you stay alert and don't space out when you relax, you can notice all this happening.

There are also many changes that we can't feel occurring in blood lactate and hormonal levels, immune system function, metabolic activity and so on, which I detail more fully in my book, *How Meditation Heals* (Ulysses Press, 2001). For our purposes here, it is quite enough to notice the obvious changes.

Our bodies, and the systems within them, continually oscillate between activity and rest. Our nervous system has the role of maintaining balance, and it operates like a thermostat. The sympathetic branch of the nervous system winds us up and the parasympathetic branch winds us down, according to the situation we find ourselves in.

In the "up" or "arousal" phase, initiated by the sympathetic system, we feel anxious or excited. Adrenaline and other hormones get to work. Muscles tighten, blood pressure and breathing rate rise, and we burn a lot of energy fast. This often feels good if it doesn't last too long. We can call this the "stress" response. In extreme forms, it becomes the "fight-or-flight" response.

In the "down" phase, the parasympathetic system reverses all of this. Adrenaline levels fade, muscles relax, blood pressure and breathing rates drop, and we burn less energy as our metabolic rate falls. This is called the "relaxation response."

Initiating the Relaxation Response Deliberately

Everybody relaxes. We all fall asleep eventually. But we often don't relax well, or deeply, or long enough, and we're often unnecessarily tense during the day. We think the process should happen naturally when we want it to, but it often doesn't. We can wait for hours, trying to let go, and still feel tense.

By meditating, you can put your hand on the switch. It means you can consciously turn from the stress response to the relaxation response when you want to. The body can start relaxing within seconds. If you know how to steer it, you can wind the body down to the point of sleep within five minutes, changing all the body chemistry on the way.

This is a very useful skill, but it works best if you know what you are doing. In other words, you need to stay alert as the body descends toward sleep. It helps to keep your hands on the steering wheel, rather than just letting go and hoping.

Meditation is very flexible. You could focus on the breath or a leaf or music or an image or a concept. Nonetheless, from time to time you'll still be aware of the sensations of your body. They're always there in the background, and you can use them to check what is happening. At any moment, they can tell you where you are on that sliding scale between complete tension and complete relaxation. They will also tell you when the process has gotten stuck part way.

Many changes occur, but these are the four main signs of relaxation I ask my students to look for: the body feeling heavy, tingling on the skin, aches and pains becoming obvious and the breathing becoming lighter.

People who are sensitive to their bodies may notice them immediately. People who are reluctant to look at their bodies may not notice them much at all. But if you do notice them, they reassure you that you are relaxing well. If you actually focus on them, they act as a biofeedback mechanism and rapidly take you deeper.

HEAVINESS OR LIGHTNESS

"My body felt like lead."

"I felt I was sinking deeper and deeper into the chair."

"My hands felt numb, as if they were fused together."

"I couldn't feel my arms (legs, body). I wiggled my fingers to make sure they were still there."

Adrenaline provides a restless, chemical charge to the muscles, priming them for action. That charge fades when we start to relax, and we lose muscle tone. For example, the face may sag, and when the neck muscles let go, the head suddenly bobs forward. After three or four minutes, the whole body seems heavy and sinks into the chair. When you notice this happening, you know you've triggered the relaxation response.

Adrenaline makes us restless, so we rarely sit perfectly still for more than a few seconds. Our subtle body movements activate nerve spindles in the muscles that send signals to the brain such as, "the elbow has moved one inch to the left" and so on.

As our body settles, those signals aren't triggered as much. The brain interprets this as the body feeling numb or light or hollow. At the edge of sleep, when the theta brainwaves appear, we may feel quite detached from the body, as if it's barely there.

If we stay conscious as we slip down toward sleep, we notice that the body tends to relax in the following sequence, with some stages overlapping: heavy, numb, still, light, disconnected, vanishing. The easiest to notice is the sense of heaviness.

TINGLING OR WARMTH ON THE SKIN

"My skin felt warm and tingly."

"My hands and feet became quite hot."

"I felt warm in the meditation. I'm cooler now."

"I could feel the pulse in my hands (neck, face . . .)."

When we are tense, the blood flow is diverted from the skin to the large fight-or-flight muscles within the body. If you are terrified, your "blood runs cold." This is what you feel when the blood has drained from the skin. Have you ever wondered in ghost stories why an icy chill announces the presence of a spook? Now you know.

The reverse happens when we relax. The blood thins out and flows back to the extremities. The skin gets warm and tingly. The skin feels alive, the same way it does after a shower or aerobic exercise or a shot of alcohol.

Usually the sensation is subtle, but for some people it is very obvious. Their hands may also get puffy and wedding rings may feel tight. People who suffer cold hands and feet are often pleasantly surprised by the flow of warmth. As one woman said, "The room temperature feels just perfect."

The improved blood circulation also loosens up congested muscles, which become more soft and pliable. People sometimes describe this as a "good energy flow" through the body. The stiff places start to soften. Many people will pick up the pulsing of the blood throughout their whole body.

ACHES AND PAINS SURFACING

"I didn't realize how tired and tense I was."

"I thought I was fine when I started to meditate. Then I noticed this awful headache and my stomach is sore too."

"It took a long time for the pain in the shoulders to go."

When we are tense we produce endorphins, which are the body's natural opiates. They numb the body out. We often feel fine when we're on overdrive because we're not feeling anything at all. This is the secret of a runner's high: stressing the body produces opiates.

When we relax, however, the painkillers fade away and we gradually notice what we've been doing to our bodies. The little aches and pains all come to the surface—sore neck, headache, itchy skin or just that total body ache of fatigue. The long-distance runner usually feels pretty awful when he relaxes afterward.

Pain is often part of relaxing. For example, if you sit down after a couple of hours' work in the garden, you'll feel quite good while the energy is still running through you. After five minutes relaxing, however, you realize you're aching all over.

This can annoy people who see relaxation as a kind of oblivion. They would prefer to leap straight from tension into unconsciousness. Unfortunately, this is the push-yourself-and-collapse cycle. It's not a healthy way to live.

It's much better to relax into and welcome the aches and pains. This is a way of making peace with yourself just as you are. Their presence is a good sign that you are relaxing. Give yourself a pat on the back.

If you fight pain, it stays or goes underground to erupt later. If you accept it, it finds its own way out of the body. It needs to surface to get free. Pain that is part of the relaxing process can in fact be quite pleasant. It is like the "good" pain you feel in a massage, when the masseur's fingers are loosening the sore spots.

A common sequence is "no pain, more pain, less pain." First we feel no pain because the stress hormones are making the body numb and we're living in our head anyway. As we relax, the discomforts surface and may be worse than we thought. By the end of the meditation, however, the headache is fading and the shoulders feel better. And by triggering the relaxation response, the loosening process continues after the meditation is over.

CHANGES IN THE BREATHING

"My breathing became quite light and occasionally stopped."
"My breathing was quite erratic. Sometimes I had to sigh or take a deep breath."
"I felt I wasn't breathing enough."
"My breathing felt deep and lovely."

The way we breathe mirrors our levels of tension and relaxation. When tense, we tend to breathe from the upper chest only, and to hold the breath. This gives us a certain charge so we can respond quickly, if we have to.

As we relax, we gradually let the breath go. When people start to meditate in class I hear little sighs around the room. The shift from tense, upper-body breathing to loose, open breathing usually occurs in jerky stages over two or three minutes.

Finally the breathing can become very light and delicate. We breathe, after all, for a reason. We need oxygen to burn energy in the cells to maintain our level of metabolic activity. Tight muscles burn a lot of energy, even if they're doing nothing. When they relax, they need less energy, so we breathe less. The breathing now feels light, delicate and spacious.

If the mind, which also burns energy, becomes very still, there can be a long pause between out-breath and in-breath. This can be a lovely moment, when the breath dissolves into space and everything seems to stop. This is when you know that peace is not just an idea. It's a physical experience, even if it only seems to last a few seconds.

OTHER SIGNS OF RELAXATION

Most people can notice the above signs of relaxation—heaviness, tingling on the skin, aches and pains, and changes in breathing. However there are also other indicators that are less common, and more specific to individual people. It is best to find out what your own special landmarks are, so you know you're on track.

For example, many people feel their stomach gurgling. Others have more saliva in the mouth. "I know I'm relaxing when I have to swallow," said one student. For some people, their eyes water or they feel a little nauseous or they become aware of an old injury again.

There are also many very real but subjective indicators—a sense of peace, or release, or flow, or stillness. I'll talk about these and other mental signs later.

Relaxation Is a Process

Strange to say, when we are tense nothing much may be happening in the body. The mind is going wild, but the body is locked up. Conversely, when we relax, the mind becomes still, but big changes occur in the body. We don't instantly switch from being tense to being relaxed. It's a fluid and dynamic process that usually takes eight to twelve minutes to complete.

We can say the body goes through three stages in most meditations—tense, relaxing and relaxed—and they are quite different in quality. Most of an average meditation is likely to be in the "relaxing" phase. This means you're watching things that are constantly changing.

For example, the breath may typically go through the following sequence. It starts short and tight, then loosens with a sigh or two, then settles down rather erratically until it feels deeper and more rhythmic. Then typically it gets lighter and slower and occasionally stops. At times, if you start thinking again, the sequence will even reverse and go back to an earlier stage.

Checking Your Meditation

First ask yourself, "Am I relaxing?" and look for the signs. Does the body feel heavy? Does the skin feel warm or tingly? Are you more in touch with the body as it is, including the aches and pains? Does the breathing feel soft? If you can answer "yes" to any of these, you know you're on track.

Then you could ask, "Could I relax some more?" And often you can. You may just need to let go of that conversation in the back of your mind or more consciously be in the moment. You may find that the body responds immediately. You drop that thought about work and something softens in your chest.

By meditating, you're trying to relax the body and get the mind clearer. At the end you could ask, "Has it worked? Am I more relaxed and less caught up in thoughts than I was twenty minutes ago?" When you meditate, it's quite enough to be moving in the right direction.

Don't hold out for perfection. You might notice that a relaxed body is not automatically pain-free or filled with bliss. It's just relaxed. Nor is a clear mind automatically happy. It's just seeing what's going on with clarity. Meditation is not a "happy" pill. If you're going through a divorce or an illness, meditation can keep you physically relaxed and mentally clear, which will help a lot. But don't expect to be perfectly happy about it all.

You can feel disappointed with your meditation for the wrong reasons. Often you're relaxed and clearer, but you still don't like the way you feel. You wanted that beautiful radiant feeling you got three weeks ago. Or you wish you didn't feel so exhausted. Even worse, you want the experiences that your teacher or your fellow students talk about.

Aiming for an ideal state is setting yourself up for failure. It's far more sensible to remember your goal: relaxing the body and clearing the mind to whatever degree is possible. If you keep that in mind, you'll know whether or not your meditation was a success.

Spot Meditations

It takes less than a minute to take the edge off your tension. In that time you can drop your metabolic rate maybe 10 percent. If you give the body half a chance, it will sink back toward balance in a flash. It takes five or ten minutes to reach total rest, but stripping away the excess tension takes almost no time at all. Spot meditations are extremely time-efficient.

We are all very good at tensing up. A coffee at breakfast starts the process. Driving to work winds us up a bit more. Then a demanding meeting or an aggravating encounter can rapidly lift our tension levels to the maximum.

But when the meeting is past, what do we do? We stay stirred up. We're not good at winding back to a more balanced state. This is where spot meditations come in. They press the "you can relax now" button.

You can do them almost anywhere: sitting at your desk, walking down a corridor, at the toilet, standing in the elevator. If you drop your metabolic rate just 10 percent, that means you burn 10 percent less energy for the next hour or so. If you do several spot meditations a day, you can keep yourself in balance all day and hardly ever shoot up into the danger zone. You won't feel wiped out at 5 pm, because you haven't burned out your energy reserves.

Spot meditations take you back to basic principles: shift from thinking to sensing, be present, just watch, focus on something sensual. A spot meditation is often just a very short version of a formal meditation.

Once you understand the principles, you can apply them anywhere. I'll offer you many more spot meditations as this book progresses. Have fun with them.

Spot Meditation: Seven Sighs

When tense, we hold our breath, and the out-breaths tend to be short. When we relax, we let the breath go. The out-breath becomes longer than the in-breath. When we completely relax, we sigh and rest for a moment or two before breathing again.

By deliberately sighing, we mimic the physiological effect of relaxation. It sends signals to the mind saying, "It's okay to relax now." Sighing is probably the fastest way to induce the relaxation response.

Don't try to force the sighs. Just let go as much as feels right each time, and wait for the new breath to come when it wants to. You'll find each sigh usually goes a little deeper than the last. After three or four sighs, the whole body starts letting go in sympathy.

INSTRUCTIONS

- Wherever you are, sigh deliberately seven times.
- Enjoy the feeling of total body release as you breathe out.
- Notice that each sigh is usually deeper, slower and softer than the one before.

- Rest as long as you like in that stillness at the end of the breath.
- Seven sighs is quite enough. Now enjoy the natural breathing as long as you like.

Body-scanning Meditations

Excellent as the breath meditation is, the body-scanning practices have even more potential. Throughout the world, you will find a huge variety of practices based on the body and the play of sensations within it.

In particular, our perception of the body changes dramatically as we relax. When we're tense, we feel the body as being hard and solid. This seems obvious, but as we relax, we feel it more as a fluid play of sensations that come and go in consciousness. As we enter the first stage of sleep, we sense the body in a dreamlike fashion as being spacious and almost empty.

This ever changing nature of the body as we perceive it is extremely useful. The sensations act as a biofeedback mechanism. As we focus on them, they become our guides and lead us deeper. We feel the body itself leading us back to balance and health.

In this practice, we scan the body in deliberate stages, from top to bottom or bottom to top. We use the changing sensations in each place—tingling, pressure, pain or whatever—to hold our attention. This tends to bring the more subtle tensions to the surface, which alleviates many of them within seconds. It is like combing the knots out of a tangle of long hair.

Body Scanning and the Breath

Obviously, this practice resembles the breath meditation. In body scanning, you focus on the body sensations while having a background awareness of the breath. In the breath meditation, you do the reverse. But there is another important difference, which is why people generally prefer one or the other.

The breath meditation is usually more tranquil. The mind ideally stays in one place and always returns to that place. There is a peripheral but not very detailed awareness of the body, which relaxes because the mind is relatively still. This suits people who prefer simplicity and stillness.

Other people find this approach boring and get easily distracted. They resent always returning to square one. They focus much better if they have something more systematic to do. Since body scanning is more active, it suits people with active minds. With more to see and feel, it keeps them occupied.

The two meditations also have different general flavors. Focusing on the gentle ebb and flow of the breath can be rhythmic and soothing. You can almost forget the body and go into slightly hypnotic states. In other words, you can be very tranquil but not very alert.

Body scanning, however, tends to illuminate all the good and bad sensations, and make you very aware of your body and yourself, just as you are, in the moment. You also notice how your thoughts impact on your tension/relaxation levels. In other words, body scanning enhances self-awareness.

The Effect of Scanning

Whatever practice you do, it is good to have a background awareness of the body. If you choose to actually meditate on the body, you get a double-whammy effect. The mind is focusing and you are also reading the effects of that immediately. The mind and body form a biofeedback loop that can accelerate the process.

As soon as you start relaxing, you notice what happens physically. The breathing loosens and the pressures of the day drop from your face. As the endorphins fade, the deeper tensions and chronic rigidities come to the surface and loosen their grip. As the adrenaline levels decline, you feel your muscles softening and your limbs growing heavy. If you scan slowly and thoroughly, you realize how each individual part of the body feels as it shifts from tension to relaxation.

With more sensitivity, you can pick up other downstream effects of the relaxation response: subtle breathing, more life in the digestive system, and a gradual sense of warmth and flow throughout. The "energy-field" (i.e., the network of sensations in the body) becomes more fluid and alive. It is easy to imagine you are nourishing all the cells of your body by just sitting still and doing nothing.

A meditator can illuminate the whole body from within. Many of my generation of meditators were taught to spend a whole hour doing one scan of the body from top to toe, or vice versa. It is extraordinary how entertaining this can be. The body is alive with sensation—tingling, pulsing, pressure, pain, bliss and the ebb and flow of the breath. It continually changes according to the activity of the mind and the depth of meditation.

By scanning you may also notice the emotions that accompany your tension. Your tight neck muscles or lower back pain may bring up feelings of frustration or despair. Chest pain or general discomfort may be interlaced with anger or resentment.

Since emotional reactivity is the basic cause of bodily tension, body scanning gives you a chance to face it. Fortunately both the physical and emotional pain tend to release if you just watch and accept them.

Nonetheless, the process often results in a deep sense of pleasure. It still surprises me that physical bliss can co-exist with the inevitable discomforts of having a human body. Some of my students even tell me that severe pain and illness are no obstacles to relaxation and mental clarity. Sometimes, they even help.

While most meditators have a reasonable degree of body awareness, some make it their speciality. Body scanning can have such extraordinary effects that I am inclined to regard it as the most powerful of all healing meditations.

But you can try too hard. Because scanning is so therapeutic, people often try too hard to relax each place and make it feel good. This rarely works and can lead to frustration. Meditation relaxes you because it is a kind of "not-doing" that is free of the effort that makes you tense.

The best quality of focus is a loving and accepting curiosity toward the body, just as it is. This is what gives it permission to relax. All you can do is focus without expectations. If the mind is settled, everything else happens automatically.

Body scanning lends itself to many variations. Here are four ways to approach it.

Meditation: Body Scanning

INSTRUCTIONS

First sit comfortably and shake your body loose, releasing any obvious tension. Take a couple of deep breaths and let go completely as you breathe out.

Scan the body at your own speed, noticing the subtle detail. You can count the breaths if you wish, spending perhaps four, or eight or ten breaths in each region.

1. Scalp and forehead
   Notice tingling, pulsing, pressure …
2. The face and lower part of the head
   Soften the eyes. Let the mouth and jaw go slack
3. Neck, throat, shoulders, arms and hands
   Like stroking or massaging the body with your mind
4. Chest and upper back
   Feel the lungs expand and contract
5. Diaphragm and solar plexus
   Feel the movement of the lower ribs
6. The belly and lower back
   Feel the soft organs move slightly as you breathe
7. Hips, legs and feet
   Feel or imagine the breath dropping through your body

Now let your mind rest wherever it wants to in the body. Watch the breath or the heartbeat or any other sensation in that place. Stay there as long as you like or scan again, either up or down. Enjoy the feeling of the body relaxing.

Meditation: Breathing Through the Body

If you have a more tactile disposition, you may prefer to imagine you are "breathing through" the body, or massaging each part of it with the breath. You can gently comb out the tensions as you go. If you can feel your heartbeat, you can imagine it gently pulsing through every part of the body as you scan.

Meditation: White Light

A common practice is the "white light" meditation. This means you imagine an almost liquid light flowing through your body. It could be a soft golden light, like nectar or milk and honey. It could be a sparkling crystalline light or a cool blue light or a warm pink light.

Be kinesthetic and feel it flowing especially into the painful places. Let the light have texture and aroma and even sound. You can amplify the effect by saying an affirmation such as "Love" or "Peace" or "Health" on each out-breath.

If you wish, you can imagine the light caressing your organs, flesh and bones. Feel it going through the brain, the nervous system, throat, lungs, heart, intestines, liver, kidneys, sexual organs, the spine, buttocks, arms, legs and feet. This "mind-massage" is a way of caring for each part of you.

Meditation: Chakras

In this meditation you let your mind rest in the central point (i.e., the "chakra") of each of the seven regions listed in the Body Scanning meditation. You stay in each place until it feels loose and open, and move on to the next. This is the process of "opening the chakras" and can be combined with an affirmation or mantra.

Supporting Your Practice

On my seven-month retreat in 1984, the circumstances were excellent. There was solitude in nature, the freedom to do what I wanted when I wanted, no books or media of any kind and no distractions but the internal ones. Nonetheless, I wondered how much my good states of mind depended on the setting. Would it all fall apart when I returned to the city?

I resolved to train myself so my meditation wasn't reliant on circumstances. I wanted to be able to meditate anywhere, on anything, with anyone and under any conditions. I've encouraged my students to be equally versatile.

However, each week someone will ask me, "Why can't I do it at home? Why is it so much better in a group?" Beginners often do need the array of nonverbal supports they get in a group or in some kind of routine. Although they know what to do, it works better if the props are in place. Because meditating is quiet and subtle, and very little is actually happening, anything noisier in our minds and lives can blow it apart. It needs protection, particularly in the early days.

In this chapter I talk about the peripheral supports that can help your meditation thrive. Though many are commonly expressed as rules—as the things you need to do to make it work—I don't see it that way. I regard them more as options. Try them out and see what works for you. And be prepared to move on if you outgrow them.

"How Much Should I Meditate?"

Just because you've done meditation in the past doesn't mean you can turn it on at will. Like any skill, it fades if you don't practice it and improves if you do. The wheels get rusty if you've missed even a few days or weeks, and your next session is likely to be ragged.

I suggest you aim for fifteen minutes, five days a week as a minimum. If you do that amount you'll be happy with your progress. Any less and you'll find the stops and starts frustrating. It takes about two months for a beginner to engrave the practice in memory. Over that period, you really get to know what works for you.

You can do that fifteen minutes in one sitting or in three or four short meditations during the day. Some people are very good at meditating in a parked car, during a lunch break in the park or in a supermarket line.

Fifteen to twenty minutes is a natural period of time for a formal sitting. Of course, longer sessions are good too. You tend to go through three stages in any meditation, which usually take about fifteen minutes. In the first stage the mind is chattering a lot. In the second, you relax rapidly and often get sleepy. In the third, you wake up a little and get the right balance: relaxed body and awake mind.

Finding the Time

People often complain, "I haven't time to meditate!" but I don't believe them. We fill our lives with compulsive activity whether we need to or not. It is the keep-busy-and-worry habit gone crazy.

One student said her life was too busy with full-time work and managing a family. She seemed so frantic I almost believed her. Halfway through the course, she gave up her job and suddenly had an extra forty hours a week. Yet she still complained, "I can't find the time."

We don't have to carve a fifteen-minute hunk out of each day. There are gaps everywhere. The trick is to notice and use them. If you ask yourself many times a day, "When can I meditate?" you'll eventually find the spaces to do at least spot meditations.

When meditation becomes a habit, like brushing your teeth, it will no longer feel like something extra that you "have to do." It only takes a few minutes, but it helps you function better, think better, sleep better and enjoy life more. Those few minutes soon pay for themselves.

"What's the Best Time to Meditate?"

There is no "best" time to meditate. Is there any time of day you wouldn't benefit from being relaxed and aware? But you will find some times are more satisfying for you than others.

Some people are larks and some are owls. If you meditate each day at a certain time that suits your lifestyle and temperament, it can be a very enjoyable habit. Here are some of the common times that people meditate.

Very early morning is delightful. Monks and nuns throughout history have meditated in the darkness before sunrise. The body's metabolism is still slow at this time but the mind is rested. This often gives a tranquil but alert meditation that lasts till the first bird calls. I find the early bird calls have an almost visceral effect on me, stirring me up for the day ahead.

Although predawn is too early for most of us, early morning is still a good time—but do wake up first. If you try to meditate in bed, you will just go back to sleep. If you have time, have a shower or brisk walk and then meditate before the rest of the neighborhood comes to life.

We can get unnecessarily speedy in the mornings with the energy of a night's sleep behind us. To come back into balance, it's good to meditate just before you leave the house. Five minutes on the couch is quite enough to reset the thermostat. Similarly, if you arrive early where you are going, why not sit in the car and meditate before moving on? I find that mothers often meditate just after the kids have left for school.

Many of my students who are business people will cut out fifteen minutes in the middle of the day. Some are quite forthright about it. They lock the office door, turn on the answering machine, and lie down on the floor or a couch. Others are more discreet, choosing to meditate in a park at lunchtime instead of eating in a noisy cafeteria.

I discourage people from meditating while driving, though I know they do it. Beginners often assume that meditation is a sleepy, blanked-out space, regardless of what I say. Obviously, this can be dangerous while driving. Also, people don't realize how rapidly they can drop from a state of relaxed alertness into unconsciousness. It only takes a few seconds asleep at the wheel to kill someone.

However, if you insist on meditating while driving, there are ways to make it safer. Don't use the breath meditation or mantra, which can be very soporific. Make "driving" your meditation object.

Focus on the experience of driving itself. Pay attention to the scenery and passing traffic, and notice what you are doing. Notice your breathing and muscular tension, but don't go too deeply into them. In other words, stay present and in touch. If you emphasize this broad-spectrum awareness rather than deep focus, you're likely to drive more safely and enjoy it more.

People often find it hard to meditate at home because of all the distractions there. They meditate better in their cars. They pull over at a park or a beach on the way home and sit there, letting themselves unwind. One woman told me she goes out to the garage and sits in the car to meditate. "The quietest place in the house," she said.

It is excellent to meditate after arriving home from work. It helps you leave work behind and reclaim the evening for yourself. You often have a messy sitting at this time, as the remnants of the day parade through, but it helps you detach from it all. It can act as a "power-nap," giving you an energy charge afterward. You find you can use your evening productively instead of crashing out in front of the TV.

If you sit before you go to bed, you'll detach from the problems of the day and won't take them to sleep with you. But don't meditate too long. Meditation will refresh you and you'll stay awake when you go to bed. Five to ten minutes is usually safe. Just get clear of the thoughts and catch that downward momentum toward sleep.

Once in bed, you can meditate to put yourself to sleep. If it's 11 pm and you're tired, two or three minutes of good focus will send you off. If you wake in the night, you can meditate to go back to sleep. The secret is to meditate well. Switching on music and listening to it carefully often works well.

Paradoxically it is best to aim for sharp focus if you wake at night. You can't waffle your way back to sleep. It is the moments of good focus that cut you free from the thoughts that keep you awake.

Group Energy

Why do people commonly find it best to meditate with others? What is this mysterious "group energy"? Any group of people that comes together for a purpose will develop a collective mood that affects them all. It's like the sum total of all their moods mixed together. We unconsciously resonate with each other's emotional states more than we think.

For example, the moment you walk into some offices you notice a poisonous atmosphere. You can feel the hostility and warfare in the air. It affects your behavior despite your best efforts. Similarly a gathering of friends can have an atmosphere that can't be duplicated elsewhere. As a result, a group of people sitting to relax and focus tend to support each other's mind space unconsciously.

This is why people get very attached to certain religious leaders. In the East, you go for "darshan," to just sit in the aura of the great man and be shaped by it. The effects of being in the presence of a teacher or other good meditators can run deep.

There's a palpable biochemistry in group dynamics, though some people don't find it helpful at all. As a good solitary meditator, for years I found the high energy of sitting in a group hard to handle at times. I now like it, but it's very different and more unruly than sitting alone.

The Setting

People who come to my center often say, "I feel relaxed as soon as I walk into the room." It is great to have a specially designated time and place to meditate. Even experienced meditators appreciate it. It helps enormously to meditate with other people for an hour each Friday night, for example.

Because of the associations, people pick up nonverbal cues from the room that trigger the feeling. It may be a smell, or something visual, or just the mind going through the memory bank saying, "I recognize this place. It's where I get into those nice inner spaces."

This will happen in any place where you meditate regularly. The sensations don't even need to be pleasant. Even the smell of moldy carpet in the church hall where you sit on Tuesday nights could give you positive reinforcement.

Similarly, you may find that insignificant gestures have strong effects. For me, throwing my cushion into the center of the floor is enough to change my living room into a meditation space. People often light a candle or incense. They may put something beautiful in their field of vision, or have some very quiet music in the background. It doesn't take much to create a supportive mood. A hint is all you need.

Other people get more elaborate. They set up a small shrine with a candle, flowers, fruit and beautiful things on it. They then have a shower and put on white clothes, say a few prayers and go into the meditation proper. They often finish with some gesture such as blowing out the candle.

If you have a choice and your surroundings are pleasant, it is best to meditate outside. Being in nature takes you away from the artificiality of modern life. On a beach or under a tree, the mind becomes more natural. Spending fifteen minutes each morning on your porch, just being present, would be a great thing to do.

How Do You Start?

It's a big leap from meditating in a group or a class, or reading a book, to doing it on your own. It helps to consciously reproduce the supports of time, place and routine in your own practice.

First choose a time. It's great if you can schedule it in your diary. An even better approach is to ask yourself repeatedly during the day,

"When could I meditate?" and try out various slots from early morning to late night.

Also ask, "Where could I meditate?" Just because your living room or balcony is an obvious place, don't get stuck there. If you ask yourself repeatedly during the day "Could I meditate here?" you may find many unexpected places and times.

When you do a formal sitting, ask yourself, "What would help?" Very simple things such as burning an essential oil, lighting a candle, or having a piece of music playing very, very softly in the background can work wonderfully. Just a single cue can be enough. You don't need to reproduce the full temple atmosphere.

Even when you start to meditate, a routine is useful. Remind yourself what you're trying to do. You could just say, "I want to relax and settle the mind," or you could have a more personal goal. Don't just sit down blindly hoping something lovely will happen.

Then go through the basics: check your posture, loosen your breathing with a sigh or two, notice the sensual quality of your environment, notice the unfinished thoughts in your head. You've now arrived at stage one: you're in touch with yourself. You take it from there.

Spot Meditation: Animal Liberation

If your day has been pure hell, and any attempt to discipline the mind seems like masochism, then try this exercise. Don't try to focus. Just practice detachment. Open the cages of the mind and let the savage beasts run riot.

INSTRUCTIONS

- Let go. Give up all effort except the effort to let go.
- Don't try to sit correctly or focus on one thing. Just watch.
- Let the wild animals run—problems, pain, fantasies and fears. Stand back and watch them. Resist the temptation to run after them, picking up their droppings.

- Every few seconds, ask, "What's happening now?" and name the strongest thought or sensation. Don't try to fix anything. Just take an inventory. Keep naming.
- Enjoy the relief of complete despair. Tell yourself you're incapable of productive thought at this moment. It's probably true, so do nothing. Be like an irresponsible parent who couldn't care less about his or her kids. Let them sort themselves out.
- At the end ask, "Do I feel any better now?"

Sound, Posture and Breath

The sounds around us are excellent to focus on. Like the breath and the body, they are always with us. Any time we meditate, we'll inevitably be aware of sounds from time to time. We notice the traffic, the air-conditioning, a dog barking, a car alarm going off, a door slamming nearby, a plane overhead and so on.

If you get annoyed and feel they're disruptive, they will be. You may occasionally be oblivious to sounds, but it's impossible to block them out completely. Hearing and identifying sounds is an essential safety function of the mind that you can't erase. It happens even when you sleep.

If you feel that silence is essential for inner peace, your meditation will always be vulnerable. You'll also feel anxious each time you sit, and resentful toward the outer world that makes all that noise. You may feel that city life is toxic by nature and you have to escape it to relax at all.

It's much easier if you can accept the random sounds and even use them to deepen your practice. After all, they don't distract the way thoughts do. They are sensory stimuli just like the breath or the sensations of the body, and they can bring you into the present.

Random sounds are good for keeping the mind bright. They remind you where you are and what you are doing. If you're getting sleepy in your meditation, you can wake up by listening to the sounds around for a few seconds. If you lose the sounds completely, it's often a sign you're falling asleep.

When I sit, I periodically check my mental clarity by noticing how precisely I can listen. If the sounds are vague and blurry, and I can't quite catch the start of a new sound, it's obvious that my mind is rather dull. It's usually a sign that my energy is being drained by some semiconscious thinking in the background.

Meditating Directly on Sounds

Meditating on random sounds is an ancient practice and one of the best. One reason that yogis have traditionally meditated in deep caves was to listen to the sounds of their own bodies. It is extraordinary how noisy the human body is—breath, heartbeat, digestion, the hum of the nervous system and so on. Furthermore, this inner symphony changes its tune as you become more tranquil.

To focus on sounds, you have to pay moment-to-moment attention or you'll miss the next sound. Although the sounds are unimportant in themselves, when you're totally with a bird call or a car horn, the past and future vanish. When you start to notice the subtle sounds you'd normally miss, you know the mind is discarding its background conversations.

Breath and body meditations have an introspective quality. They take you inward and often make you overly aware of your discomforts. Sounds, however, take you out of yourself, which can be a relief. You may be focusing on things that are hundreds of yards away. You also realize you don't have to shut the world out to relax. You only have to be passively aware and "just listen" to it.

Random sounds give you a sense of space. When you hear one sound to the left and another far behind, and you notice the space between them. Sounds also tend to disappear. If you are totally focused on a sound that vanishes, the mind is suddenly alert but empty. The same happens if it's silent and you're waiting for the next sound.

Soon you realize this sense of space and emptiness can be very stable. You can be totally alert though focused on nothing. It's not a mental blankness, since you'll notice the next sound immediately. This apparent emptiness is in fact the background consciousness through which all your thoughts and sensations pass. It is the screen on which your mental dramas are projected.

Stretching the Basic Instructions

Meditating on random sounds seems to be stretching our basic instructions about focusing on one thing. In fact, the "one thing" can be anything you choose to direct your attention to. In this case, it is the entire soundscape, which is made of hundreds of individual sounds. It resembles the body scan meditation, in which you focus on an array of different sensations in sequence.

Similarly, the "meditation object" could be the sensation of swimming, or the activity of cooking a cake, or the storyline of a visualization. All these things have clear boundaries. When you meditate, you basically put a fence around something and explore what is within the fence. The fence could be huge enough to embrace the whole soundscape. Or it could be quite tiny—the breath at the point of the nose, for example.

The purpose of focusing is to deflect the mind from chronic thinking. When you notice you've jumped the fence and are following some thought, you stop and return to what you were doing—listening, swimming, cooking, visualizing or whatever. Random sounds are a good example of a large and varied meditation object. The fence can be huge, so long as you know when you're inside it and outside it.

Meditating on Music

Music is an excellent meditation object. It holds our attention well and leads us along in time the same way an instructor's voice does. If you lose it, it's easy to find it again. Being sensually rich, it draws you away from thought.

Yet there are problems with it. Few of us are used to listening carefully to music. We commonly use it as sound wallpaper, or drift along aimlessly with it, letting our thoughts go where they will. While this may be relaxing, it won't lead to mental clarity.

With any meditation, no matter how pleasant, there needs to be an element of discipline and self-awareness. You know what you're focused on and you know when you've wandered away from it. Without conscious focus, you won't be able to detach from your thoughts. In this practice, you notice when you're really with the music and when you've gone off at a tangent.

Meditating on music should be like going to a concert. You can be relaxed but also alert. If you've paid $50 for a ticket, you want to hear what you've paid for. You don't want to space out for two hours. And you find that if you listen carefully, you enjoy the music more.

Stages of Depth

Any meditation will take you through stages of depth, and these are quite obvious when you listen to music. At first the music seems to be somewhat distant and doesn't penetrate the cloud of habitual thoughts around you.

Then the music breaks through and you're affected by its mood. Many people get images and associations, but none of these need to be a distraction. It is all part of the meditation object—i.e., the musical experience—unless you go off at a tangent with it. To check, you can ask yourself, "Am I still with the music?"

Just occasionally, we become so absorbed in the music we are aware of nothing else. We forget ourselves completely for just a few seconds. This is when the music seems to become exceptionally beautiful. This is a state of oneness, or absorption, or what the Indians call "samadhi." Enjoy it while it lasts.

What Kind of Music Should I Use?

People often assume you need spacey relaxation music to meditate to, but this misses the point. It is the focusing, not the music, that does the work of getting the mind clear, and it doesn't even matter if you like the music or not. After all, you don't have to aesthetically enjoy random sounds to use them as your focus.

Almost any music will do if it holds your attention. Recently a man told me, without a shred of irony, that he meditates to the frantic jazz of John Coltrane. I also find that fast complex music, like Bartok string quartets, draws me in and keeps me focused well. The music you use could be fast or slow, tranquil or passionate, simple or complex, classical or New Age or planetary. It is your choice.

There are just two exceptions to this. Vocal music can get you thinking about what the singer is saying. And some New Age music is deliberately fluffy and insubstantial in order to make the mind space out. You need something clear enough to focus on, so you know when you've wandered away from it.

Ambient Music

You can also use music to set a mood without actually focusing on it. In other words, you focus on the breath but with soft music in the background. Obviously, you will notice it from time to time in much the same way as you notice random sounds, but it's not your main focus.

One advantage of ambient music is that when your mind wanders, it tends to fall into the music rather than into thoughts. The music acts as a safety net. Another advantage is that the sensual and usually rhythmic qualities of music augment the sensory component of your meditation.

The music you choose needs to be quite bland. Anything dramatic or even musically interesting will distract you from the breath. CDs of nature sounds or relaxation music are quite suitable.

Finally, the music needs to be played very quietly—about half the usual volume or less. When we meditate, our hearing becomes very acute. The music should be so quiet that it doesn't dominate consciousness. It should be like the random sounds—something that you notice in passing and occasionally don't notice at all.

Meditation: Random Sounds

INSTRUCTIONS

- Relax the body and the breathing as usual.
- Tune in to the soundscape.
- Don't reach after sounds. Let them come to you.
- Notice the little background sounds you would normally ignore.
- Try to catch a new sound the moment it arises.
- If the mind wanders, come back to the next sound
- Enjoy the texture and color of sounds. Listen to them as music.
- Follow sounds to the end. Enjoy the emptiness when they vanish.
- When it's silent, enjoy the space as you wait for the next sound.
- Periodically check your body to make sure that you're actually relaxing.
- Remember, you're doing something very simple: just listening.

Meditation: Music

INSTRUCTIONS

- Settle the body and the breath as usual.
- Switch on the music and enjoy the color and detail.
- Let it resonate in your body.
- If images or associations arise, blend them in.
- Ask yourself occasionally, "Am I still with the music?"
- Notice the special live quality when you're 100 percent with the music.

- Let the mind slow down and go into the fine detail.
- When the music stops, come back to yourself.
- Did you relax fully, or are you still a little charged up?
- Spend the last few seconds in silence.

Posture and Breathing

If I mention the word "posture" in class, at least one person will shuffle guiltily and attempt to "sit up straight." Posture is important, but it is much misunderstood. For example, many people never attempt to meditate because they assume they have to sit cross-legged on the floor.

In fact you can meditate in any posture. The four classical Buddhist postures are: sitting, walking, lying down and standing. There are several variations on each of those, and then you work with the postures in between. Since the aim was to be relaxed and aware all day long, you couldn't just do the practice sitting.

What matters is not the posture but how you hold yourself in it. In any posture, you should be comfortable (but not super-comfortable), balanced and open (so your breathing isn't constricted), and alert. You can't expect to meditate well slumped in an easy chair or curled up in bed. The general rule is: don't slump. If you sit against a wall, it's best to have a small cushion in the small of the back.

Good posture actually grows from within as you become more aware. The best way to find good posture is to notice the moment-to-moment sensations of your body. Do you feel tight, hard and locked-up? Or loose, open and balanced? If you let your body adjust itself during the meditation, good posture will develop automatically.

Sitting in a Chair

In 1995, I was at a conference with 150 meditation teachers from around the world. I imagine every one of us had learned to meditate sitting on the floor. However, at the conference about half of them were now meditating in chairs. Of course some of them had ruined their knees, pushing through the pain barrier all those years ago in Asia. But for most of them using a chair just worked better.

Most Westerners find a straight-backed, padded office chair is ideal. It should be low enough to have both feet firmly on the ground. If you are short, put cushions under your feet. Even better, cut the legs of the chair to the right size. This is worth doing if you plan to meditate a lot. Most chairs are designed for the average man and are too high for many women. I had two inches cut off the legs of half the chairs at the meditation center.

Some people like armrests, and some don't. These can prevent the shoulders slumping and prop you up. They are good for the elderly and infirm, and they're good for you at any age, if you happen to be feeling that way.

When sitting in a chair, the right-angle between torso and thighs can block the breathing a little. You can overcome this by spreading your legs apart and letting the belly hang out. This creates a tripod effect with your two legs and your bottom. This "samurai" pose doesn't look very "feminine" but it supports your lower back well.

Sitting on the Floor

This is an excellent position if you are relatively supple and fit. Otherwise, it takes strain to hold and you tend to slump. After a few minutes, the lower back balloons out and the shoulders collapse. This blocks the breathing, compresses the inner organs, and inhibits the vitality of the body.

Slumped shoulders induce a slight feeling of depression, a kind of "leave me alone" mood. If you let your shoulders slump right now, you'll notice what I mean. It is like lying half-asleep in bed when you don't want to face the day. People who meditate a lot, especially those in religious groups, can fall into this trap. They can shut down their bodies and minds and go into a slightly depressed, escapist state of mind.

To sit well on the floor, you need *big* cushions that get the hips well above the knees. Zen practitioners use solidly padded cushions that are a good eight inches deep. These can be large enough to tilt forward slightly when you sit on them. Some people like myself put a smaller cushion at the back to increase the tilt. This throws the hips forward, supports the lower back well and opens the front of the body so you breathe easily. It is like sitting on an ergonomic chair.

Sitting without a back rest gives you a sense of independence and self-reliance. It also allows the body to move spontaneously and adjust itself internally. The "energy" moves up and down more freely than if you're leaning against a chair, which is important in more advanced stages of practice.

If you're too old and stiff to start sitting cross-legged (i.e., after about thirty for most of us), you can use a kneeling stool. This is just a narrow plank about two feet long by four inches wide. Legs at each end hold it about ten inches off the ground. The plank is usually tilted about 30 degrees forward to open up the hips. Your legs go underneath in kneeling position. These stools are surprisingly comfortable. This position has most of the same benefits as sitting on a cushion.

Reclining Chairs and Lying Down

To use a reclining chair, or to lie down, usually means you're willing to go to sleep. It can be quite hard to stay awake when your body is totally supported. Most meditations in this position will be a little vague. However, this position is excellent if you're elderly, or if you suffer neck and back problems, or if you're too sick to hold an upright position without strain.

It is also good for people who suffer chronic anxiety. They need all the encouragement they can muster to help them unwind. Being able to relax consciously is so important for their health and well-being, they can concentrate on just that aspect of meditation. The mental clarity can come later.

Using a reclining chair is also good if you're just too tired to meditate otherwise. This can often be one meditation in every four or five, given the lives we lead. The meditation then becomes like a short conscious nap to revive yourself. This is well worth doing even if it seems rather slack.

Finally, you could meditate lying in bed with an alarm clock. The body is biologically designed to go into a rest phase, if not actual sleep, once every ninety minutes. If you make sure you wake after fifteen minutes, you maximize the benefit of that resting phase without wasting the afternoon.

On retreat, I let myself snooze whenever I feel like it, like a cat. I set the alarm and meditate to drop into sleep quickly. I often wake before the alarm goes off fifteen minutes later. I might do this four or five times a day. I find this keeps me fresh and dispels those sluggish patches. It also means I sleep less at night and get up about four or five in the morning.

What Is Good Breathing?

If you can "just watch" the body and the breath, without trying to control them, they will find their own way toward balance and health. But can you watch the breath without trying to control it? And what is good breathing anyway?

When you watch the breath, you rarely find it perfectly fluid and easy. There may be subtle blockages everywhere. As you relax, these start to loosen automatically. In other words, you don't have to "do" anything. Just noticing is enough.

Relaxed breathing is often quite erratic—now shallow, now deep, occasionally stopping. If you've ever watched a healthy baby sleeping, you've probably noticed their breathing is rhythmic and flowing and luxuriously indulgent. No wonder we wish we could "sleep like a baby." But even this healthy breathing is still not perfectly regular. You'll notice the odd deep sigh, jerky patches and times when the breathing stops altogether.

The same happens in meditation when you are deeply relaxed. This kind of breathing feels healthy and perfect, yet it can be quite different from what we think of as "good" breathing. It's loose and spacious but not necessarily regular or deep. It is changing in response to subtle shifts within body and mind.

The Need to Control

Many people are quite anxious about the natural activity of their bodies. They wonder if they are breathing "correctly," and feel they should control it to "make it better." Some people even try to control their heartbeat as well.

They may not realize how much they fear and try to dominate their bodies, since the habit builds over decades. Some people hold themselves very tight, attempting to control the uncontrollable. Others are more trusting and sympathetically listen to the needs of their bodies. One person learns meditation because "I want to *make* myself relax." Others are willing to *let* themselves relax. The latter usually do better.

As an infant grows, it soon finds certain emotions are too overwhelming or socially unacceptable to be expressed. Emotions ride on the breath and tend to move up or down through the body. Anger and joy move upward, for example, and sorrow and fear move down. The easiest way to suppress them is to cramp the free flow of the breathing. The blockages most commonly occur in the throat, the chest and the diaphragm.

If the emotion never releases, the control has to stay in place to keep it down. Breathing is stiff and jerky. Many people find the breath quite uncomfortable to focus on—perhaps because of the monsters behind the locked doors. Much tension comes from the struggle to suppress unwanted emotion.

Meditation should be a gradual loosening of unnecessary control. However, just as the entrenched bureaucrats of former communist states want to stay in control, so does the nervous system. If chronic anxiety and workaholism have got you where you are today, you are naturally reluctant to give them up. Your doctor tells you to relax, but your conditioning says, "No! Hang on!"

Controlling the Breath Can Be Useful

Ideally we just let the breath flow the way it wants. In practice, the blockages can be too strong to dissolve naturally, and controlled breathing can help loosen them. For example, you could do some yogic breathing exercises, or just try to make your breathing deep and rhythmic at first. Even simpler, you could take a few deep breaths and sigh at the start of any sitting.

Controlling the breath like this can focus the mind well, but it's still a control mechanism. It is good to go the next step and let the breath be free. Relaxing should be like sleep. We don't control the breath when we sleep, nor do we need to control it when we relax.

Nonetheless, I find about a quarter of the population will always try to control the breath. It's just their nature. This is not a problem so long as they control it as little as possible, like gently holding the reins of a horse. It's quite okay to smooth the rough edges of the breath and round off the turns. Finally, when the breath becomes extremely fine in states of deep tranquility, it is actually hard to say whether we are controlling it or not.

Control is not automatically "bad" and freedom "good." We need a little of both, though we tend to err on the side of control. Christianity emphasizes man's dominance over nature, and even for those who are no longer outwardly Christian, that attitude can still cast its shadow when they meditate. They feel they should impose their will on the breath and the body. They just can't trust it to do the right thing.

The Eastern assumptions are different. It is assumed that nature can be trusted and that the body is wise. The homo sapiens model has been around for millions of years, and it knows how to breathe. If you get your interfering mind out of the way, it will do exactly what it needs for health and balance. Good posture, breathing and lovely states of mind, emerge naturally from within, if you let them. All you have to do is sit still and watch.

Spot Meditation: Red Light

I took many radio interviews when the original edition of this book came out in 1993. The interviewers were fascinated by the idea that you can meditate in the forty-five seconds you're stuck at a red light. In fact, a television team invited me to fly across the continent to Melbourne so I could demonstrate.

A team of eight with a backup truck met me at the airport. The car had a camera mounted on the hood, pointing to the driver's seat. It was a gray winter's day, so there were bright lights within the car itself, shining up on my face. So I drove off into rush hour traffic, late on a dismal Friday afternoon, to demonstrate the red light meditation.

This exercise works best if you are running late and the traffic lights turn red as you approach.

INSTRUCTIONS

- If you feel frustrated, smile at yourself.
- You have been given a whole minute to stop and do nothing.
- Relax. Shake yourself loose and settle back in the seat.
- Take a deep sigh or two, lingering on the out-breath.
- Look around you slowly. Notice exactly where you are.
- Scan your body for excess tension. How are you holding the steering wheel? Are your face and neck muscles tighter than they need to be?
- Let the belly soften. Take one whole minute to breathe softly.

This exercise finishes as the lights turn green. Now devote all your attention to the task at hand: driving safely. And look forward to the next red light.

Awareness, or "Watching with Detachment"

Meditating is typically described as a balanced pair of opposites: relaxed and alert; calm and clear; body asleep, mind awake; tranquility and awareness. Occasionally it is defined as just one side of those pairs, as "one-pointed focus" or as "continuous awareness," but this feels incomplete. Meditating, and the mind itself, is paradoxical in its nature.

Even the core instructions are in two parts: "focus on one thing, and watch other thoughts and sensations with detachment." This involves two separate skills, focusing and watching. Focusing seems to be the more important. It's certainly what you try to do first. But it soon breaks down unless you can also watch with detachment.

Even the results of these two skills are different. Focusing lets you escape your thoughts. It takes you out of yourself and into your object. It ultimately leads to deep tranquility and the trance states. It gives you the relaxed, calm, tranquil side of that pair of opposites.

Awareness, or "just watching," however is more subtle. It disarms the troublesome thoughts. It grounds you in your body. It allows you to see your body, mind and emotions dispassionately, rather than just escaping them. It gives you the alert, clear, aware side of that pair of opposites.

There is no doubt that focusing is simpler to understand. It's also easier to do and more sensually enjoyable than watching. As a result, people commonly neglect awareness. They do it only with reluctance when they are forced to acknowledge distractions in their meditation. Typically they want to "just get rid of the thoughts," so they can feel good. This is not a recipe for success.

Focusing is your initial strategy, but the quality of any meditation depends more on how well you relate to your ongoing thoughts and feelings. They'll be with you every time you sit and all your life as well. You can't escape them for long, and you'll never come to the end of them. Furthermore, the way you respond to them changes according to what they are and how tense or relaxed you are. Awareness is a complicated skill.

What Are the Other Thoughts and Sensations?

Meditation seems to divide the world into two. There is the meditation object and all the rest. This seems simple enough. You're just trying to focus on something sensual and let the other thoughts and sensations pass in the background. Why is it so hard to stay on track? And why do thousands try and give up in disgust?

They get distracted, of course. The "other thoughts and sensations" seem to be, and actually are, more important than the meditation object itself. It's not surprising that they call our attention. Let's have a look at what they consist of.

To help us do so, we'll use a model of the mind as a stream of consciousness, since we perceive thoughts serially, one after the other. It's easy to imagine these thoughts as objects floating downstream, successively coming into view and vanishing from sight.

In meditation, it's impossible not to notice things other than the meditation object. A dog barks, a cough starts up, you think of yesterday, the body feels sore, a memory flits by, you feel tired and bored and find yourself wondering, "What will I eat tonight?" These are the most obvious things floating downstream.

That's not all. You're half-aware of other concerns: your sick mother or delinquent son, a lingering feeling of unwellness, conflict at work, concerns about cash flow or inadequate retirement funds, your golf game getting inexplicably worse.

On top of that, the media or our daily conversations may trigger off more mental activity. We are vaguely alarmed by environmental degradation, the stupidity of our leaders, the rapid approach of ageing and death, and those too-hard questions such as "Who am I and what am I doing here?"

No wonder we get distracted and feel stressed. That stream of semiconscious thoughts and feelings is the ultimate source of our anxieties. Annoying as it is, it also gives us our memory bank, our sense of self, our ways of understanding and evaluating the world, our imagination and drive, and it's our ultimate source of pleasure.

Yet meditation seems to trivialize it all by saying, "Focus on one thing and let everything else pass by." Does the breath really deserve more attention than everything else put together? Why on earth do we focus on it at all?

Focusing Helps Clear the Mind

None of the background thoughts and sensations are inherently bad. It's just that we get overwhelmed by their sheer volume and emotionality. When we're being swept downstream by the deluge, we need to get out to be able to deal with them at all. This is where focusing comes in.

You can't sort things out if you're caught in the stream. It won't work. You have to clamber up on the bank to get any perspective at all. You do this by focusing on a vantage point in the distance and gradually moving toward it.

At first the vantage point (i.e., the breath) seems remote and insignificant. As you approach it, it becomes clearer and larger. Soon you can sit the mind down on it and it stays there. Anything we pay attention to puts other things behind us, just as going to a movie or partying with friends makes us half-forget our difficulties at work.

Important as the breath is as a safe haven, it's not all that interesting in itself. The truth is that we focus, not for its own sake, but to see our thoughts and feelings more clearly. This is where your meditation bears fruit.

Once you're outside the stream, you can turn around and look at it from a distance. You notice exactly how sick, healthy or tired you are, and the mood you're in. You also see the issues in perspective. It now becomes obvious what dress you should wear, what to say to your delinquent son, and how to schedule your activities tomorrow.

Awareness Develops in Stages

It's relatively easy to know whether you're focused or not. You just have to ask, "Did I feel that last breath?" and it will be obvious. Furthermore, the body relaxes rapidly when you focus well so you know you're doing it right. Awareness and the art of detaching from thoughts, however, are more complicated. It's not just a matter of "getting rid of" thoughts by naming them. Furthermore, it passes through several stages.

The starting point is where you are unconsciously caught in a chain of thought without even realizing it. This happens much more often than we like to admit both in the meditation and out.

The first stage of awareness is where you at least know what you're thinking about. This is where you can say, "Oh, I'm thinking about Sally." You're still immersed in the thought, but you now have the choice whether to stay with it or not. This is when it is useful to "name the distraction."

To extract yourself from Sally, you try to focus on the breath. At first Sally protests and doesn't want to let you go. Furthermore the breath feels weak and distant. At this stage, you're often halfway between the two, half thinking and half focusing.

Even when you get a good grip on the breath, Sally may or may not go away. She's quite likely to hover in the background, feeling rather neglected but still calling you. You can't let your guard down. Stay with the breath and tolerate her presence.

When you were caught up with Sally, you probably didn't notice anything else. Thoughts tend to obsess us and make us blind. Once you're settled on the breath, however, you're quite likely to notice peripheral things as well: sounds, sensations in the body, the quieter background thoughts and feelings in the mind. The mind feels more spacious.

You are now meditating quite well. You are focused on the breath and noticing other thoughts and sensations with detachment. And the stream really does bring new things down every second. You have to keep an eye on it or you're likely to get sucked in.

People often fall into a trap at this stage. They let themselves go so deeply into the breath that they don't notice the stream any more. Unfortunately, this usually results in a decline in awareness. A sign of this is that they get shocked by external noises. Typically, they are calm but almost asleep and out of control. Nice as it is, you can't go any farther from this state.

Paradoxically, the way to go deeper is to enhance peripheral awareness. I check my quality in the deeper states by checking how clearly I can hear the surrounding sounds, whatever they are. I alternate focusing (on the heartbeat, in my case) with peripheral awareness (of the sounds), aiming for high quality in each.

Once you get stable in that edge-of-sleep state where the theta brainwaves arise, the passing thoughts and sensations cease to be distractions at all. In theta you feel dissociated from your body and your usual sense of self. The peripheral activity doesn't stop, but there is space between you and your thoughts. The mind is in neutral. The gears don't mesh with the passing thoughts.

You are now able to consciously examine the stream itself. Initially you had to turn your back on it and keep your eye on the breath to get onto the bank. Once you're free, rested and on dry land, however, you can turn around and look at it with dispassionate curiosity. It's not so much of a danger now.

It is fascinating to watch this subtle interplay of feeling, sensation, image, memory and thought from the outside. The usual inner dramas are still played out, but they're less compelling now that you've now left the stage and are in the audience. When you're free of your habitual anxiety and desires, healthier mental qualities emerge: curiosity, interest and pleasure.

First you see more deeply. You see yourself and your mental dynamics in more detail from this new perspective. Then you notice things you'd never seen before—dream imagery, fluctuations in mood, subliminal dialogues, deep pleasure and timelessness.

Now you can take awareness one step further. You might pluck something out of the stream and deliberately focus on it. You might focus on a dream image or a passing mood or a memory or a pain or the texture of consciousness itself. The usual instructions apply: focus on the object (i.e., a dream image or a pain) and let other thoughts and sensations pass by in the background.

Finally, you can even let the instinctive mind guide you. Typically it will ask you to focus on a physical or emotional pain that needs to be identified, but ultimately it will take you anywhere. This resembles daydreaming but is utterly different. You are not at its mercy in the least. If you find your emotions getting engaged, you can drop back to a clear, focused mind in an instant.

To summarize, awareness goes through various stages from the starting point of unconscious thinking. They are: noticing what you're thinking about; pulling away from the thought; focusing while tolerating background thoughts; freely watching passing thoughts and feelings; consciously choosing to focus on a thought or image that arises; letting the deep mind guide you.

Also notice that the early stages above occur in beta, the middle stages in alpha and the later stages in theta. The way you practice awareness depends on the stage you're in. You can't, for example, let the mind lead you (a theta option) when you're battling obsessive thoughts (a beta state). So let me describe in more detail how you develop awareness in beta, alpha and theta.

Beta: Naming the Distractions

While you meditate, the mind is continually oscillating between focusing and watching. For example, you focus on the breath, then notice a bird or car, then return to the breath. The mind moves from the meditation object to "the rest" and back again.

While in beta, focusing is more important than awareness. It is both your sanctuary and the vehicle that takes you there. It is the way you escape the compulsion of thought and start the inner journey. You turn your face to the object and your back to the stream. You can't compromise on this.

To find your way to the vantage point of the breath, you also have to notice the obstacles in the way and how you're coping with them. This is where you name the distractions—"work . . . food . . . headache . . . sadness . . ."—with the primary aim of extracting yourself from them.

Alpha: Watching with Detachment

As you focus better and relax more, the thoughts are less of a problem. They're less sticky. You're more able to watch them with detachment. Nonetheless, unless you're vigilant, you'll soon fall back into them.

In alpha the quality of thoughts change. They become less obsessive and more random. They break up more easily and often slip laterally into daydreams. Since they hog less space, you often notice the periphery more—the sounds, sensations in the body, memories and your changing mood.

Even though they are not the meditation object, it's important to be aware of these. They tell you what's happening in the moment and act as biofeedback mechanisms, taking you deeper. You still have to stay on guard against temptation. The mind is still oscillating from the object to the rest, but "the rest" is not the problem it was when you were in beta.

Theta: the Free Mind

Once you move into theta, both focusing and awareness change again. On the sleep threshold you detach from your usual sense of body and self anyway. You no longer have to focus to escape the compulsive thoughts, since they've largely disappeared. You focus to stop yourself from falling asleep or getting lost in fantasy.

If you're clear and stable in this state, however, focusing is almost irrelevant. It's easy to do and for safety's sake it's good to continue with it, but it takes almost no effort. Focusing is critical for getting through beta and alpha, but in theta the other half of the equation, awareness, takes over.

Initially theta is a pleasant, half-asleep state oblivious to thought. We could call this "dark theta." With more awareness, it becomes more steady and serene. Let's call this "tranquil theta." The more you can consciously recognize this feeling, you more you know how to protect it and deepen it.

Finally theta wakes up and becomes lucid. The stream of fine thoughts, sensations and images that now appear in "lucid theta" is spectacular, yet so subtle that you could fail to notice it for years. It's in the twilight zone between waking and sleep, and we're just not accustomed to noticing at all.

In lucid theta, your awareness has no limits. It's not confined, as it was in the early stages, to identifying distractions to get free of them. In this state, you're free to focus on things that arise. You can ask, "What is this?" Or other words, "What is happening right now?" You can consciously examine the subliminal images and feelings in the mind.

The Zen Ox-herding Pictures

A series of ten educational pictures from ninth-century China illustrates the stages of development in a meditator. I'll use the middle ones to illustrate the shift from beta to theta. Imagine a wild black bull rampaging through the jungle with a little boy chasing it. The bull represents the totality of the mind. The little boy represents the ego that tries to control it.

Once the boy has caught the bull and put a noose round its neck, he drags it out of the jungle toward a post in a clearing. In other words, he pulls the mind away from riotous thinking toward the meditation object. And it is a battle!

Once the bull is tied up, it leaps around trying to escape but eventually sits down and rests by the post. It watches the jungle from a distance (alpha) and eventually falls asleep (theta).

Once the bull is tamed, the little boy can untie it and ride on its back. He now takes it back into the jungle and directs it where he wants it to go. This is where you can consciously examine what arises in the mind without getting lost.

Eventually, the bull is in harmony with the boy, who no longer has to control it. He throws away the harness. He sits on the bull, facing backward, playing a flute. The bull goes freely through the jungle, following its instinctive animal wisdom.

In a single meditation, the balance between focusing and awareness shifts the deeper you go. In beta, focusing (or tying the bull to the post) is crucial and awareness basically plays a rear-guard action, battling the distractions. In alpha, focusing and awareness are equally balanced. In theta, focusing is almost effortless, and awareness takes over. The spade work has been done, and the mind is free to explore.

Awareness Is a Practice on Its Own

Though awareness is part of any meditation, it is also a practice on its own. People tend to gravitate toward the awareness pole of that focusing-awareness spectrum as they become more skilled, and it is obvious why.

Focusing keeps your eyes on the road, but awareness lets you enjoy the scenery. Almost all the satisfaction of a sitting comes not from watching the road but from those sideways glances at the scenery. The physiological shifts, the bodily tranquility, the pleasure of mental freedom are all part of the scenery. When you're focused, you only see the breath.

Since awareness is already part of every meditation, the instructions are unique to it. In an awareness meditation, you don't have any new object to focus on. It's more about shifting your emphasis when you meditate from focusing to watching, from spotlight consciousness to floodlight consciousness. You become a spectator.

In most meditations, you focus inwardly on the meditation object. When practicing awareness, you do the opposite. You still have a focal point, which could be anything at all, but most of your attention goes outward, "just watching" the passing thoughts and sensations.

When doing a formal breath meditation, for example, you would only notice other thoughts and sensations when they grab your attention. When practicing awareness, however, you may still be focusing on the breath, but you allow other thoughts to surface. You deliberately watch them pass through consciousness.

You try to keep the mind neutral. You aim for a bland, mirror-like mind. You don't think about what is happening. You don't chase good things or resist bad ones as you usually would. You just notice what has walked in the door this minute and let it walk out again. As you can imagine, this doesn't come easily. Some visitors are very seductive.

A Typical Awareness Meditation

Let's assume you are meditating at the end of a busy day. You start in a beta state, tangled in thought. You soon realize you're thinking about Sally and work and money and a bunch of other stuff. These semiconscious irritations won't go away if you try to ignore them. They have to go out through the front door. As you name each thing, you break free somewhat and the breath is easier to focus on.

Then you realize Sally is back. Naming wasn't enough to get rid of her. This isn't surprising since she's been bugging you all day. The tangle of irritation, sadness and recriminations behind your inner dialogues now become obvious. Once you register your feelings and can see that further thinking isn't going to help, it is easier to let them go.

Notice that awareness doesn't solve the outer problem. It just changes your reaction to it. You stop fighting the imperfections of the moment and just let things happen. You feel a twinge of back pain; a motorbike goes past; you notice annoyance (you can't help it), and feel the annoyance fade; your breath feels soft and lovely; you feel anxious about money; then you realize you're thinking about the earthquake in Peru. And it's all okay if it just flows by.

On a larger scale, awareness means being comfortable with an uncomfortable world. You may tend to feel that you can't relax until the problems are all sorted out, but this is an unhealthy attitude. Issues around relationships, identity, money and so forth will go on for decades. You can't plan to relax when you're sixty-five, because stress will probably kill you first.

Not All Distractions Are Equal

Awareness is complicated because of the huge variety of things that go through consciousness. Some have a high emotional charge and some have a low one. It's easy to watch the pain of a slight headache. The pain of a bitter divorce is a different matter. It's even harder to just watch things that are gnawing at you unconsciously.

Each time you get distracted, you have a little challenge. Can you tolerate this without annoyance? Can you stay passive? The first strata of distractions are usually sensual things such as pains in the body or noises outside. Pretty soon you realize these don't need to be a problem. Being sensual, you can focus on them temporarily without breaking the meditation. If a tickle in the throat or a plane going past is the most obvious thing in the mind, why not focus on it for the time it's there?

However, you can't focus on thoughts this way. You can safely go into sensory things, but you have to pull back from thoughts. At the same time, you can't block out or ignore them. They do carry important messages and need at least a moment's attention. Usually by the time you label them, the mind has already assessed their importance and whether you can afford to drop them or not.

Being able to name your thoughts—"Stephen, TV, work, Paris"— will disarm most, but not all, of them. Often a thought won't let you go till you face the feelings behind it. If you chronically overeat, "food" can be too superficial a word to identify what's going on. Or if you're worried about a drug-addicted daughter, saying "Angela" doesn't encompass the matter.

If naming the content of a thought doesn't do much, then try naming the feeling behind it—despair, or desire, or misery or contempt, for example. This will give a fuller picture. Often you can't think of any single word that fits. However, just to let the feeling register in consciousness usually quiets it down.

Notice that naming the thought or feeling is not complicated at all. It's just putting single word labels on to the dramas. Also, you're not avoiding them, as you do when you try to focus on an object. Since naming a thought is much cleaner than endlessly running stories around it, it saves energy and the body relaxes.

Shifting the Balance from Focus to Awareness

After you break the dominance of thoughts, awareness becomes quite easy and natural. In the alpha zone, you can balance focusing and awareness. You can be with the breath half the time and watch the stream for the rest.

You still have to be vigilant, but as the body settles, you get even more freedom. It becomes possible to watch the show as a spectator. This is how focusing, which is so important at the start, gradually gives way to a tolerant and versatile awareness.

As you watch what flows downstream, you become familiar over time with its huge variety and the way it changes as you relax. This is actually "you." It is the texture and contents of your mind. You become able to watch every last thought, sensation, feeling and image, just as it is, without being entranced by it. You also see how it connects causally: how a thought leads to a feeling, which leads to a response in the body and often to action as well. These are some of the fruits of awareness that make it worth cultivating.

Meditation: Awareness, or "Just Watching"

Naming is the basic technique when you practice awareness, but you do it sparingly. Don't try to name everything. That would keep you very busy. Don't go looking for anything. Just name what is obvious and notice the rest without naming it.

Nonetheless, naming isn't essential. It's just a device to help you watch things with detachment, which is the real purpose of this meditation. If you are watching dispassionately, you don't need to name. Many things are too complex and subtle to be named anyway.

Originally I didn't enjoy naming and rarely did it. It felt like an unnecessary imposition. Only in recent years have I discovered how useful it is to precisely identify what is happening. Being able to name what's in the stream, even if you rarely verbalize it, can greatly refine your awareness.

INSTRUCTIONS

- Relax and focus on any meditation object.
- Make good contact with it. It is the seat from which you watch the stream.
- Every few seconds, name the most obvious thing in the mind, whether it is important or not: "sore knee ... hungry ... TV ... money ... traffic...."
- Don't lose contact with your basic meditation object. Spend at least half the time with it, and check that you're actually relaxing. In fact, go as deep into the object as you can without ignoring the peripheral thoughts and sensations.

- Notice how the scenery changes the deeper you relax.
- Notice that when you wait for thoughts, they often don't come!
- Enjoy the bland, impersonal quality of the clear mind.

PART THREE

The Secondary Practices

Mantra and Affirmations

Whatever you meditate on, you'll still have some awareness of your breath, your body, sounds and thoughts. Every meditator has to relate to these in some way, and of course they're great to focus on in their own right. These are the "bedrock" practices of the previous lessons.

So when you meditate on something else, you don't leave them behind completely. While focusing on a candle or a mantra, you will still have random thoughts, you'll hear the traffic and you'll feel your body. Since you can't block them out, you include them in the meditation.

It's very easy to combine meditations. They mix well. Since you can't avoid hearing sounds while focusing on the breath, why not focus on both, alternating from one to the other? Similarly you can scan the body while saying an affirmation, listen to sounds while doing your yoga or add a beautiful image while watching the breath.

To keep the instructions simple we say "focus on one object," but in fact several objects can work even better. It helps a lot to have secondary points of focus. You're not "distracted" when you move from the breath to a candle to a sound. They're all sensual things that keep thoughts at bay.

In the chapters that follow, I'll build on the bedrock of body, breath, sound and awareness meditations. I'll give you other things to focus on, such as mantra, affirmations, visual objects and images. I'll also

introduce walking and other active meditations so you can relax anywhere and anytime.

The underlying principles don't change, but once you understand
them, be creative. Notice that you can turn simple things you do each
day—eating a cookie, having a shower—into opportunities to relax
and get the mind clear. And even within a formal meditation, notice
what actually produces the best results for you. See how far you can
bend the rules. Even the best students play up at times! When you
know how to play the piano, you can jazz it up and improvise.

Mantra Is a Very Simple Practice

Awareness, the subject of the last chapter, is a sophisticated practice.
Mantra is just the opposite. It is so simple that it is rarely "taught" at
all. You are usually told, "Here. Say this mantra." And that's all there
is to it.

A mantra is a word or a phrase that you say over and over, often
in time with the breath. It's a stripped-down form of chanting. It is
like an affirmation, but affirmations have meaning and mantra often
don't. Or the meaning they have is secondary to the sounds.

Mantra are musical. Each has its individual rhythm and sound
quality, and people frequently sing them. It can be a sensual, hypnotic
and absorbing practice.

Here are some common mantra:

OM

HAMSA (and its opposite, SOHAM)

OM MANI PEME HUNG

OM NAMAH SHIVAYA

HARE KRISHNA

OM AH HUNG

Mantra Can Be Said Many Ways

Usually people say their mantra silently, or "think" it, like an inner
chant. They often blend it with their breathing to enhance its rhythmic

qualities. A mantra is very easy to hold onto. Once you get a mantra ticking over, it becomes a soothing hum or resonance in the body.

Hindus often sing their mantra. Hinduism has a great tradition of popular sacred songs called "kirtan" and "bhajan." People sing these simple and beautiful songs for hours at a time, and the boundaries between mantra and devotional singing become indistinguishable.

People often dance to their mantra, as we know from seeing the "Hare Krishnas" in the street. Since this takes a lot of energy, it is regarded as a good practice for young and undisciplined minds.

In India, mantra are often said very loud and fast. You occasionally see a holy man marching through the streets shouting his mantra. This is the high-pressure hose theory of mantra. It blasts everything else out of consciousness.

People often start by saying a mantra out loud. As they relax, the mantra fades to a murmur and merges with the background hum of the body. Eventually the mantra stops of its own accord and the person rests in stillness. In the deepest states there can be no words at all, not even mantra.

The Historical Background

The word "man-tra" literally means "mind-tool." The "tra" actually is the Sanskrit root of the English word "trade." It really is a tool for the mind to hold onto. It is a vehicle to take you deeper.

However "mantra" also means "a magical spell." Of all the practices in this book, mantra carries the most religious and mystical overtones. It comes from the "abracadabra" era of human thought, when sounds were believed to have magical effects.

The earliest Indian texts we know of were basically collections of invocations and spells. The priests could say mantra to make the sun rise or the rains come, to protect you from disease, to destroy your enemies, to ensure the favor of the gods, to make your neighbor's wife fall in love with you, or in more modern times, to make your child pass his exams. Who said that meditation isn't useful?

Because the spells had to be said exactly right to work, a whole priestly caste emerged. They were the specialists in mantra and the associated rituals and sacrifices. We can be forever grateful to those brahmins who said the correct mantra this morning to make the sun rise.

The pseudoscientific explanation for this is that each sound has a certain vibration that triggers off specific effects in our bodies and the world around us. As usual, there is a grain of truth in this. Sounds do have individual effects. The mantra "Ah," for example, drops through the body like a sigh. If you said it thousands of times, you would become as loose as a beanbag. Though meaningless, it still has an effect.

The mantra "Hung," on the other hand, resonates in the chest like a bell, and holds in the energy. In contrast, the mantra "Hree!" seems to shoot upward and lift your energy. It is clearly not intended to help you relax. Each mantra, therefore, has a different mood and effect which is amplified when you repeat it thousands of times.

Different religious groups often identify with particular mantra. They are like badges of allegiance or slogans. Furthermore, though the mantra may be meaningless, they do tend to carry associations.

Tibetans use OM MANI PEME HUNG, which evokes one's sense of friendliness toward all living creatures. Siddha Yoga uses OM NAMA SHIVAYA, which evokes one's inner wisdom, symbolized by the god Shiva. Hare Krishnas use the 32-syllable HARE KRISHNA mantra, which may bring to mind Krishna making love to the cowgirls. And groups tends to claim their mantra is the best.

Mantra without Trappings

These associations can make mantra seem religious or superstitious, so both Asians and Westerns have attempted to strip mantra back to its essence as a chant. Every culture uses chanting. Almost any word would suffice. You don't need one sanctified by thousands of years of use.

Benson in *The Relaxation Response* suggests using the word "one" as a mantra. LeShan in his pioneering book *How to Meditate* suggests picking two syllables by opening the phone book at random. Rational as this seems, I find that most people prefer the traditional mantra. There is something about their rhythm and sound quality that works well.

The Transcendental Meditation group (TM) came out of India in the late 1950s and set the benchmark for mantra practice. They claim their practice is a no-nonsense psychophysical discipline, and have helped enormously in making meditation respectable in the West.

Because their practice is so standardized, it lends itself to scientific testing. Like McDonalds hamburgers, every TM practitioner around the world does much the same thing. Most of the independent research on meditation has been done on TM for precisely this reason. Researchers love it.

Nonetheless, TM has cleverly exploited the magical associations of traditional mantra. Since each sound has a unique vibratory effect in your body, they argue that you must use exactly the right sounds for you personally. (They don't say what would happen if you used the wrong sounds. Perhaps your liver would explode, or you'd go insane!)

Fortunately, they happen to be the experts in such things. For a few hundred to a few thousand dollars—the price is usually based on your income—they will give you your personalized mantra in an initiation ceremony. You are forbidden to tell it to anyone, and you meditate on nothing else from that time on (unless you sign up for graduate courses).

So is TM a con? It has some cultist aspects. It is expensive. It has its own internal metaphysical language. It has an enlightened master at the top. It claims to be the one true way and is contemptuous of all other practices. If you sign up, you are encouraged to be faithful and, in fact, believe. And it has created a multibillion-dollar empire.

Yet despite the hype, TM is just an ordinary mantra practice. It probably works well for that third of the population that temperamentally is suited to using mantra. What price can you put on peace of mind? Many TM people have gotten their money's worth a thousand times over. If it is expensive, people are more likely to practice and therefore get good results. If they believe that TM really is a technique of special power, they will activate the placebo effect and it will work well for them.

But do mantra need to be personalized and secret? After all, this is the only distinguishing feature of TM as a meditation practice. In the East, mantra are in the public domain. They are written on walls and printed on clothing and heard each day in the streets and temples. They're in popular songs, on the fronts of buses, engraved on rocks and fluttering from flags. Kids know them before they can read. There is even the reverse myth that the more people say a mantra, the more powerful it becomes.

Millions of people are saying mantra this very minute. It is a very popular and effective practice. TM is out on a limb in saying you need a personal mantra. It flies in the face of evidence, since personal mantra are rare in the Indian tradition. Millions of people over thousands of years have had excellent results using "ordinary" mantra.

Most people who know anything about meditation look askance at TM's emphasis on a personal mantra. It looks like a marketing ploy to justify the high price. Usually the only people impressed by TM's claims of superiority are those who are new to meditation and who have nothing to compare it with.

Mantra and the breath meditation are the two most widely used meditations in the world. Most people have an immediate affinity for one or the other, though they frequently use both in time. The breath meditation is more cool, analytic and down-to-earth. It leads to clarity of mind. Mantra, despite the many attempts to demystify it, is still more emotive and hypnotic in effect. This is just the nature of mantra.

Mantra is an exceptionally simple practice at heart. It is just a quiet chant that sets up a flow of sound within you. The images and associations that go with it could be useful, or they could just clutter the mind. It is best not to regard mantra as a magical or spiritual incantation. It is really just a "tool for the mind"—something to hold onto, just like the breath.

Meditation: Hamsa

There are many two-syllable mantra. They fit the breathing easily: one syllable on the in-breath, one on the out-breath. Generally you breathe normally and let the syllables fit the length of the breath. If the breath is long, you stretch out the mantra. If it's short, you contract it. If you try to breathe too regularly, you may hyperventilate.

HAMSA is a sensuous mantra. If you want, you can imagine the mantra (and the breath) as a wave, ebbing and flowing from your feet to your head and back again. You can imagine that you are massaging the body with sound or caressing pains and tensions in the body. First you say the sound. Then the sound takes over and carries you.

If you just focus on the breath itself, you tend to notice the individuality of each breath rather than its rhythmic qualities. Mantra, however, make the breath seem more rhythmic. Like any rhythmic activity—walking, swimming, singing—this is soothing to the mind. It counteracts the restless, grasshopper nature of thought.

A mantra is just a meditation object like any other. The same rules apply: focus on the mantra and watch other thoughts and sensations with detachment. Occasionally, a mantra can have a hypnotic effect that makes you blind to your surroundings, but this isn't its purpose.

Meditation: Om Mani Peme Hung

The problem with two-syllable mantra is that as you relax and your breathing slows down, you can drift away—especially in that space at the end of the out-breath. The most famous mantra are usually longer and said faster. They give you more to hold onto and usually have a good rhythm as well. They are commonly eight or ten syllables long, though some are thirty or a hundred syllables long.

Perhaps the most famous of all is the Tibetan six-syllable mantra, OM MANI PEME HUNG. It seems to consist of four little words, but it's usually said as a three-beat. The accents fall on the second, fourth and sixth syllables: "Om-*ma*-ni-*pe*-me-*hung*.

The formal spelling is OM MANI PADME HUM, and it is often pronounced this way. Meditators tend to blur the corners so it flows better. The mantra is usually said quite fast with no pauses and as a continuous patter, unrelated to the breath: "Omanipaymayhung omanipaymayhung omanipaymayhung."

This has a lovely rolling triple-time beat to it. It becomes a continuous flow of sound with an energizing feel, quite unlike the ebb and flow of the breath. One student said it is like sitting in a train hearing the wheels go over the tracks.

It is possible to say this mantra in time with the breath, but very few people do. It loses the forward momentum that is so much a part of its character. A few people, myself among them, say it in time with the heartbeat. It is most commonly said as a continuous hum, independent of either heartbeat or breathing. It is like a bass note in your body—easy to hold on to and easy to return to if you lose it.

Tibetans commonly say it out loud but very quietly. If you go to a temple where there are lots of Tibetans and hear a humming sound like thousands of bees, you now know what it is. Tibetans will also say it while working or walking. One student told me of hearing it used as a work song. He was following porters carrying salt up a mountain. They were saying the mantra in time with their steps.

Mantra tends to have associations rather than meaning. This one is a "heart-opening" mantra, designed to evoke a feeling of friendliness toward yourself and all living beings. The Dalai Lama is expected to manifest this mind state. It's part of his job description, and he does it well. A visualization associated with this mantra is to imagine your heart opening like a flower and the warm light of your affection spreading to others.

Affirmations

An affirmation is a word or a phrase that you say repeatedly through the meditation, often in time with the breath. Like counting, this gives the mind something to do so it doesn't wander off track. An affirmation can have the same chant-like effect as a mantra but usually carries more meaning.

Affirmations "use a thorn to extract a thorn." They use words to stop words. The continuous flow of sound can block the airwaves and stop other words from taking over.

Here are some affirmations:

- SLOW DOWN
- LET GO
- PEACE
- RELAX
- LET IT BE
- BE STILL

It is best to find your own affirmations. Any word or phrase that evokes a good feeling will do. If you enjoyed your recent holiday in Bali, you could use the word "Bali." The name of an absent lover or grandchild could suffice. A short phrase from a poem or a song could work well.

Affirmations can set a mood quickly. You can add more color to the breath meditation by saying an affirmation instead of counting. It can be like a mini-instruction, reminding you what you're trying to do. If you are getting uptight at work, just saying the words "let go" a few times as you breathe may do the trick.

Don't Focus on the Meaning

The problem with affirmations is that you're inclined to think about their meaning. Of course, this takes you back into thought, which can be no help at all. And it certainly doesn't help to regard affirmations as orders from the mind to the body.

Affirmations work best as a backup to the breath or to the body scanning meditations. In other words, you meditate on the breath but, instead of counting, you say an affirmation. It's a support that adds an encouraging mood, but not the main focus of the meditation.

Meditation is ideally a "word-free" zone. Affirmations, however, are halfway between thinking and sensing. They do involve words and ideas, but very few of them, and they don't chatter on the way our thoughts usually do. Repeating a single word or short phrase hundreds of times has a chantlike effect that tends to squeeze out more unruly thoughts. Of course you're still aware of their meaning, but I suggest you use them more as sonic wallpaper or ambient music, rather than as a springboard for thought.

Thinking about Your Affirmation

So what kind of affirmation is best? A short or a long one? A simple one or a beautiful and spiritually uplifting one? It depends on what you want to do. Tranquility and mental clarity is actually a subtle and rather unspectacular state. It takes a while to acquire a taste for it. If this is your goal, however, then the simpler the affirmation the better. Complex ideas won't let you go into that space beyond words.

Of course, affirmations are often used as a vehicle for thought. In the Christian and New Age traditions, you relax and contemplate an inspiring idea, often with visualizations included. People use affirmations to combat negative thoughts and reprogram their behavior, as a kind of direct cognitive therapy.

Thinking like this while you meditate can be very useful. It will be more in touch with your deeper feelings and intuition. It will be a slower kind of thought, with more lateral associations and unexpected insights. If you do it at the edge of sleep, you may even start "thinking" in imagery and feeling as well as words.

Useful as this is, it is still a kind of thinking. It inevitably involves some tension and effort. When you're pursuing some thought for personal satisfaction or gain, there is bound to be some sense of "I" and some kind of unfulfilled desire. The deep states of meditation are quite different—clear, spacious and effortless.

People who actively try to evoke beautiful thoughts and images in order to relax often have indifferent results, particularly if they're anxious. It's not much different from normal thinking. They'd get better results if they relaxed first by focusing on the breath or using a simple chantlike affirmation. Thinking has a place in meditation, but it's best to get the mind calm and clear first.

Meditation: Affirmations

It is easy to combine affirmations with the breath meditation. Single-word affirmations are usually said on the out-breath. Two-word affirmations obviously fit the in- and out-breath. Even longer affirmations can usually be woven into the breathing.

Still, it's not essential to blend an affirmation with the breathing. You could focus on any sensations in the body, or the sounds around or music. But don't focus on the affirmation itself. It's likely to trigger a lot of thinking, and you won't relax much.

INSTRUCTIONS

- Settle the body and let your obvious tensions go.
- Feel the ebb and flow of the breath within you.
- Say the words "slow down" as you breathe. Say the word "slow" on the in-breath and "down" on the out-breath.
- Let the words blend with the natural breath. If the breath is short, then shorten the affirmation. If it's long, then stretch it out.
- Let the breath carry you along. You could imagine it as a wave that ebbs and flows from your feet to your head and back again.

- Let the affirmation set the mood. "Slow down" enough to catch the end of each breath. Don't hurry the in-breath. Let it come when it feels right to do so.
- Stay aware of your body to make sure you're relaxing. Watch the peripheral sounds and thoughts with detachment.

Beta and Alpha Brainwaves

Our thoughts can affect our bodies instantly. When you meditate, you may notice that certain thoughts are like the tail that wags the dog. Some act as stimulants, putting us on red alert. Others are like sedatives, dissolving tension within seconds.

Exciting or anxious thoughts are like sparks that start a brush fire. Their function is to stimulate the fight-or-flight response. In other words, your energy levels shoot up, you burn your reserves fast and soon you feel rather tired.

You can avoid this stress-exhaustion cycle by letting yourself relax when you need to. The body goes through natural ninety-minute cycles of high and low energy during the day. If you deliberately rest in the lows instead of trying to muscle through them, you'll conserve energy and you won't feel exhausted at the end of the day.

You don't have to formally meditate to relax. You can actually start the process within seconds. You only need to shift from thinking to sensing, from thoughts of the past and future to sensations of the moment. Or, to put that another way, you shift your brainwave activity from beta to alpha.

Beta and Alpha Brainwaves

When you relax, the electrical activity in the brain changes. While you can't see this unless you're wired to an electroencephalograph, it's good to know about.

When you are thinking, the brain emits what are called beta brainwaves. These are between 14 and 30 cycles per second and look like choppy water on a graph. Their agitated, jumpy lines even look like the way we think.

When we are relaxed or in sensing mode, the brainwaves settle down. They become bigger, slower and more rhythmic. They look quite lovely and even serene on the graph. These are called alpha brainwaves and are between 7 and 13 cycles per second.

In the beta state we think. In the alpha state we feel and sense things. In beta we are tense and burning energy. In alpha we are relaxed and conserving energy. During the day we alternate beta and alpha. We need both, but we tend to overdo beta and ignore alpha.

Beta is not all bad. It is an active, responsive state of mind. We are in beta most of our waking day. It enables us to think, talk, handle many different stimuli at once and speculate about past and future. It is associated with the left side of the brain, which handles analytic, linear, critical thought. We need beta. It gets things done.

Nonetheless, beta is usually powered by low-grade fear, anger or desire. You may be afraid things won't work out, or angry about what is happening. Perhaps you feel you have to do or get something or you won't be happy. This is our everyday, self-oriented drip-feed of fear, anger and desire. It is exhausting and burns out the energy reserves. At some point we feel tired and start thinking about a coffee break. The mind naturally wants to drop into alpha—the relaxed, sensing, inactive state—to rejuvenate itself.

If we ignore this impulse, the mind often switches off anyway. Despite our drive and extra cups of coffee, the fatigue sets in. We go into mentally blank patches for minutes at a time—often about late morning or two o'clock in the afternoon—before recovering somewhat.

Shifting Voluntarily into Alpha

The alpha state is the natural antidote to a busy mind. When you feel tired and can't think well, alpha is reappearing. When sensing outweighs thinking—when biting into an apple or listening to rain, for example—you are shifting into alpha. When you feel an emotion in your guts rather than verbalizing it, you are in alpha.

Alpha is a state of "being" rather than "doing." It is intellectually simpler and more grounded than beta. You may not sparkle verbally in alpha, but you know where you are and how you feel. If you check, you'll also realize that your body is less aroused and you're burning less energy.

The switch between thinking and sensing happens very rapidly. When talking to a friend you will be in beta. If you simultaneously try to listen to music in the background, you won't be able to get into it. Your brain is in thinking, not sensing, mode. But if you said, "Let's listen to this song," the difficulty would vanish. Within a few seconds, your brain could shift into alpha and enjoy the music.

You bite into an apple and the taste floods your mouth. You are right there and in alpha—a moment of pleasure and relaxation. The first mouthfuls are delicious, but then you think, "These are great apples. I'll buy some tomorrow." This will take you back toward beta and the next bite won't taste so good.

Just Be More Sensual

You don't need to sit for half an hour a day in formal meditation. That's just practice. It's not the real thing. It is like doing the scales and never playing the music. All you need is to spend less time thinking and more time sensing.

Being more sensual can also make you happier. Meditators in general are happier people not because they've found peace but because they enjoy life more. They have more gaps between the thoughts. They taste their food, feel the morning wind on their faces, notice the sunset and enjoy the touch of another person a little more than most.

Like most of my students, my days are busy. I relax before my evening classes by walking in the park. I watch the native birds flit through the flame trees sipping nectar. I feel the moisture in the air after a winter shower. I watch the sun's rays flash out from clouds. These are the best moments of the day. They are also the fruits of thirty years of meditation.

An Escape from Which Reality?

People sometimes ask, "Is meditation an escape from reality?" Certainly when we relax into alpha, the world looks different. If to "be in touch with reality" is to worry about things that haven't happened, to fret over things that can't be changed and to react with panic to daily events, then the answer is, "Yes. Meditation is an escape from all of that."

A person who is chronically tense will see the world through the beta state of mind. This is the reality of money, work, superannuation, getting the kids through school and the Gross National Product. It is fueled by unresolved fear, anger and desire. We can live entirely in this state if we want. We could call it an active, thought-dominated, "male" reality.

A person who can easily relax, however, sees the world differently. In alpha, the concerns of the past and future vanish. We are more alive to sensation and feeling. We feel okay where we are and don't anxiously long for things to be different. We could regard this as a passive, sensation-dominated, "female" reality. When we stroke a cat or enjoy an apple, are we really "out of touch with reality"?

When we fall asleep, we enter yet another reality. Dreams are real to us when we are in them. Are they a complete illusion just because they don't match waking reality? So which is real? The beta or alpha or dream perspective? Is one more more important than the others?

Because meditation enhances alpha reality, it can be disturbing for people who operate on adrenaline. They can't imagine being relaxed while awake. It is as if their bodies only have an on/off switch, and relaxation can only mean sleep and oblivion. In class, I see such people collapse into the sleep zone within seconds of starting to relax.

You may even feel it is dangerous to relax. If you relax, you won't be able to cope and your life will fall apart. You could lose a grip of yourself and might even turn into a zombie. I used to receive anonymous Christian tracts through the mail warning me of these dangers.

Using Meditation to Escape

In fact many people do meditate and turn to a spiritual path to avoid facing their problems. When people can relax deeply, they often resent the outer world they have to return to. They feel the demands of children and work are undermining their spirituality. "If only I could meditate all day," they think. "If only I could go to India and be with the Teacher always. . . ." Or, "If only I could lead the pure life, I would progress inwardly."

This antagonism toward ordinary life is encouraged by many religious groups, both Eastern and Western. Cults in particular encourage an infantile dependency among their followers and demonize the world beyond the walls.

At the micro level of a single meditation session, some people also try to escape reality. Although meditation should be an alert state, as you relax deeply it can be hard to stay awake. Some people enjoy this lack of clarity and get good at sitting in a torpor. They don't quite fall off the chair, but they are barely there. It is a calm state, which is why they enjoy it, but also anesthetized and rather dull.

Some meditators get stuck in this state for years. They say things like, "I can switch my mind off whenever I want to." Or they feel good if they space out for half an hour without knowing where they are. This is called "dead-stump" or "bronze Buddha" practice. It looks good but nothing is happening. It is one of those seductive side-alleys that meditators can get stuck in.

Even good meditators have a sneaking fondness for oblivion and actively seek it at times. And in fact it's not a bad thing to do occasionally. It is quite healthy to be this relaxed, and often it's all you're

capable of at that moment. It's a good place to visit but a terrible waste
if you go there habitually.

Meditating with Eyes Open

To stop my students from getting addicted to drowsiness, I suggest that
they meditate occasionally with their eyes open. I look for this as a
sign that tells me a student is maturing. I notice them occasionally
opening their eyes for a minute or two during a meditation to coun-
teract sleepiness. Or I find them doing a whole meditation with eyes
open. Or they sit comfortably for the first or last two or three minutes
with their eyes open. I know these people really understand that meditation is "a relaxed and *alert* state."

Many people find this idea absurd at first. They say, "As soon as
I open my eyes, it's all over." They feel it's impossible to relax unless
they shut the world out and fall into a fuzzy torpor.

Others want to know why they should be able to meditate with
their eyes open. "It's so much easier with my eyes closed," they say.
Many come to classes simply to relax, and it is a real achievement for
them to do so quickly and consciously. It's invaluable for insomniacs,
those who suffer extreme anxiety and those who want to switch their
minds off.

Nonetheless, there is a long list of reasons why open-eyed meditation is good. First, you can meditate anywhere, anytime, and no
one notices. You can calm the body and clear the mind in a bank line
or a boring meeting or a waiting room, on public transport or while
walking or doing exercise or housework. If you have to keep your eyes
closed to meditate, your possible times and places are very limited. It
remains something you have to do in private, like getting undressed
or going to the toilet.

Second, you realize that meditation is not a secretive inner state
that only grows in seclusion. Open-eyed meditation counteracts the
navel-gazing tendency and vague hostility toward life that meditators
can fall into. Once you know how, you can de-stress and return to a

calm, clear state at any time during the day. In fact, life isn't hell. It's just a matter of how you respond to it. You don't have to escape to meditate.

Third, you can meditate on things of beauty. Flowers, candle flames and crystals are common things to choose. In the Asian tradition, you could also focus on a tree, clouds, the wind in the grass, the colors of a sunset, a bird in the scrub, sunlight sparkling off water, a dead leaf, a spider web or the night sky.

This increases your sense-pleasure and empathy with nature. You see more deeply. People often say things like, "I don't think I've ever looked so deeply before at a rose (crystal, flame, driftwood, apple, blade of grass . . .)." The fine-grained detail of life emerges and a new world unfolds.

Fourth, your meditation practice can become much more interesting. Meditating forever on the breath can get tedious. A lifetime focused on just one thing is not good. While it is true that the chaotic mind needs discipline, you don't need to be masochistic about it. Meditation should not be a state of pious, even penitential, boredom.

Fifth, being able to meditate on different things means you do understand what meditation is about. Many groups and traditions want you to focus on just one thing forever. They say, "This mantra has a superlative effect. Nothing compares with it." If you feel you have to use just this mantra or only breathe in a certain way, it keeps you dependent and can lead to exploitation.

But meditation is not about focusing on the breath or a mantra or any one object. It is about focusing as a skill in itself, and you should be able to focus on anything. It is about directing your attention where you want it to go. This both settles the mind down and sharpens your vision.

The Benefits of Wakefulness

Each meditation has an aftereffect. If your meditation is relaxed but foggy, that fogginess can continue. You find you're just "not there" for several minutes afterward. While closing your eyes and relaxing is useful, it's even better if it leads to clarity of mind. A clear mind is like having clean spectacles, and this effect lingers after the meditation is over. You can calmly and deliberately see what is happening around you and act appropriately.

People say things like:

"When I come in here after work I never notice the park. But when I leave, the trees look so alive and beautiful."

"I always study better after meditating."

"After I meditate, all my senses are heightened."

"For the first time, I could see what was happening between me and my daughter."

Meditation changes our lives for the better not just because we relax more and sleep better, but because we wake up and see what is happening. We are in touch with the physical sensations and emotions of being alive. For better or worse, it puts us in touch with reality.

Spot Meditation: Going to the Toilet

It's quite relaxing to go to the toilet. At least one sphincter has to relax completely or it's not worth going there at all. And when you let one muscle go, others can relax in sympathy. Furthermore, the toilet may be the only place all day where no one will disturb you.

The Buddha was the first person to recommend urinating as a meditation object. This practice is at least 2500 years old. A psychologist friend reminded me of this recently. He says he goes to the toilet in the five minutes between clients and lets *everything* go along with the urine. He gets so relaxed in those few seconds, he says, that he can barely hold his balance.

In Western literature, it is surprising how often going to the toilet is regarded as an opportunity for deep contemplation. You sit down and settle into your body. You relax, wait and randomly survey the state of the nation. Not surprisingly, bright ideas can pop up, and you feel relaxed for minutes afterward. An excellent meditation!

INSTRUCTIONS

- As you approach the toilet, get out of your head and into your body. Feel the pressure in your bladder.
- As you start to urinate, close your eyes and sigh deeply.
- Feel all the muscles of the body loosening in sympathy.
- Don't hurry to finish. After the last drop, stay motionless for a few seconds more.
- Walk away with a smile on your face.

Deeper States: Going into Theta

We have all seen cartoon images of the perfect meditator. He sits with perfect posture on a mountaintop, oblivious to the cares of the world. His thoughts, if he has any, are blissful and radiant. He seems light years away from you as you try to meditate in your untidy bedroom, tired and irritated after a day at work. "I'll never be able to meditate!" you think, as you succumb to one aggravating thought after another.

Most meditations take place with an awareness of peripheral thoughts and sensations, but occasionally we drop beyond all that. We get a taste of something special and unique and think, "That's what that yogi on the mountain feels like!"

These beautiful states usually occur at the edge of sleep when the metabolism slows down, the body becomes perfectly still and the last thoughts dissolve into the surrounding space. It is usually the moment before oblivion.

This sleep threshold state is exquisite but difficult to hold. When the body goes to sleep, the mind usually follows. By losing consciousness, however, we stumble at the threshold and miss the deeper states of mind. Good meditators are able to stay alert as they cross into the dream state, and eventually into the states beyond dreaming. They don't stumble.

Recognizing Theta

The sleep threshold is technically called "stage one sleep." This is the first of four sleep stages, each of which has its own signature brainwave pattern. Stage one sleep is when the slow theta brainwaves take over from the faster beta and alpha waves of the waking mind.

This state is also called "paradoxical sleep," because it's not quite sleep or wakefulness. In fact, it's often an oscillation between the two. One part of you wants to collapse into sleep while the other part is trying to remain awake, and you wobble between them. On an electroencephalograph, you can even see the struggle between the alpha and theta waves. If you're battling to stay awake in a boring meeting, for example, you're going into theta, or stage one sleep.

Ninety percent of the time we are in theta we're foggy or unconscious. But sometimes we're more alert than usual, and this is when it gets beautiful. It doesn't happen only when you meditate. Occasionally, when you're waking from a light afternoon sleep, the mind feels delicate and fresh. For a few seconds there are no thoughts at all. You are conscious but may not even know where you are or what the time is—delightful!

You may notice this lucid theta state occasionally as you fall asleep at night. When you first lie on the bed, you are in thinking mode. As you relax, you shift into alpha and sensing mode. You feel the sheets against your skin and the body feels softer as the muscle tension subsides.

As you relax more, you start to lose contact with your body. You may know you are still awake but not know if you are lying on your left or right side. You don't know if you're touching your partner or not. Your body is disappearing, bit by bit, as you surrender to the depths.

Yet you can still be conscious. You are not inert or dead. You still feel the subtle vibrations of life within you—spacious, tingling and warm, like the humming of the cells—which seems to be everywhere and nowhere. It has a mood also, which is something like, "God, this is lovely!" Then you fall asleep and lose it.

People often enter this "body asleep, mind awake" state when I guide meditations in class. Afterward they may say, "I seemed to be asleep but I know I was awake. I heard every word you said." Or they say, "I could hear you talking but you seemed very far away."

I teach many beginners, and as they relax, they naturally start to fall asleep. Each time I say something, it wakes them up and pulls their heads above water again. So they relax, then pull back, relax and pull back. Eventually the oscillations become small and controllable, and the meditator can balance on the edge. As one woman said, "I must have fallen asleep (and woken up) about fifty times."

This ability distinguishes a good meditator from someone who just relaxes when he "meditates." Back in the alpha zone as you start to relax, you have a choice of two paths. You can follow decades of habit and subside toward sleep. You may not quite fall off the chair, but your "meditation" will be little more than a pleasant torpor.

Alternatively you could stay awake as the body goes to sleep. This gives you the best of both worlds. It is not an either/or choice. If you stay awake, you get deeper relaxation and more mental clarity. When you can hold this state, it becomes serene, clear and timeless. You have entered the palace of the gods.

Part of the beauty of this state is that thoughts have virtually disappeared. People often ask me in frustration, "How can I block my thoughts? They're driving me crazy!" There are only three good ways that I know of.

The first is to become intently absorbed in something sensual. The second is to disengage from thoughts the moment they arise, by "just watching" them. The third, which is the most blissful of all, is to keep the mind awake as the body goes to sleep.

Letting Go the Self

Usually we are either awake, and therefore aware of self, or asleep and unconscious of self. There's a third possibility, though. On the sleep threshold you can forget yourself (as you do when you fall asleep) but still retain consciousness. There is awareness, but no awareness of self. For this reason, the sleep threshold is the first of what are called the "transpersonal" states.

If this seems rather mystical, let me explain it this way. The daily cycle from sleep to wakefulness and back again is also a cycle from self to non-self. When awake we have a strong sense of who we are and when asleep, almost none. Furthermore, we have a heightened sense of self when we're anxious, and the reverse when we're deeply relaxed.

People who are extremely anxious, paranoid or depressed assess the least sensation, thought or experience in terms of "Is this good or bad for me?" Their thoughts compulsively revolve around their problems, and they barely notice the world beyond. Their universe rotates around "I."

A person who is psychologically healthy, or just more relaxed, is less preoccupied with self. He or she can enjoy things that don't directly relate to personal well-being—music, another person, the beauty of an autumn day. He also sees his problems with more detachment.

At the sleep threshold, the sense of self dissolves enormously. It is like "a little death"—a term the Elizabethan poets used to describe orgasm. It is delightful to forget yourself so utterly and yet be awake enough to enjoy it. A good meditator, like a good lover, can protract this pleasure instead of letting it vanish in an instant.

Thinking is driven by the habitual emotions of fear, anger and desire, which keep the body aroused. Just to be awake always involves some anxiety, since we are always looking out for Number One. We can't fall asleep unless we let go of that orientation to self. The "body asleep, mind awake" state occurs when we abandon that emotional drive.

This is a colossal relief. If you remain awake, there is just pure awareness, with no agenda. Both the self-oriented thoughts and the sense of self have gone. The feeling is best described as a delicate ecstasy. It is "ec-static" in its literal meaning of "standing outside" oneself.

Of course, sleep also makes you oblivious to self, but staying awake in this state is even better. In sleep, the thoughts continue on underground and agitate the body unconsciously. If you are awake on the threshold, however, any arising thoughts dissolve instantly and the body becomes extremely still. Your metabolic rate may drop to its lowest point within minutes. It might take hours to reach this stage in normal sleep with its underlying turbulence. This is why meditation, minute for minute, relaxes the body more deeply than sleep.

As the body relaxes, it releases pent-up energy. Many people use meditation like a health-food bar to give them a boost during the day. We usually spend this extra energy on thought or action, but we can reinvest it into the meditation. If we do, we get a mind of crystal clarity and split-second awareness to accompany the physical tranquility.

Most of us could do with more sleep than we get, so we have a strong compulsion to fall asleep whenever we can. People don't quite believe me when I say it is better to stay awake. That seems like quite a sacrifice for something they can't imagine. I find people can't take my word for it. They have to repeatedly taste this state before they realize its value. It usually takes several weeks of classes before they choose to be awake rather than semiconscious when they relax.

From Tranquility to Awareness

When you first go into theta, you tend to oscillate between wakefulness and sleep. Particularly if you are tired, you will bob in and out a lot. You may suddenly "wake up" and think, "Where was I the last few seconds?"

As you get more stable, the body gets very still, and this feels good. The mental quality, however, can still be rather vague. I personally feel this state as being like a soft mist in moonlight, or like moonstone or white opal.

You can remain in this soft tranquility if you wish, but as the body becomes more rested you have another option. You can let the mind explore its surroundings. In other words, you shift from being predominantly tranquil to being predominantly aware. This doesn't break the tranquility. In fact, it enhances your awareness of it. But the awareness opens up new worlds in your meditation.

In particular, you may notice what is called "hypnagogic" imagery. This first appears as rapid and very strange dream images and memories—an ambulance roosting in a tree, a dog discussing mathematics, for example. The images differ from "normal" dreams in several ways. They tend to be extremely quick. You can get dozens of images in a second. They're often more bizarre than normal dreams. Even less than in dreams, they lack an ego-reference, or an "I" that watches them. They often come in nonvisual forms as well—as sonic or tactile hallucinations—and also contain fragments of intense thought.

Furthermore, despite their extraordinary complexity, they're extremely subtle and easy to miss altogether. It is like watching the vast complexity of the brain at work. It is quite possible that this is exactly what it is. Do these images represent the thousands of neural exchanges in the brain each second?

When people first notice these little dreams, it shocks them back into wakefulness. They know it's a sign they've lost control, and they've certainly lost their meditation object. But with skill and practice, you can get stable in this dream state. With only a residual sense of yourself and your body, you can still stay in control. Like Ulysses strapped to the mast, you can enjoy the song of the sirens without becoming their victim.

The hypnagogic state is worth exploring for its enchantment value alone. However, as you become more stable in this state, its quality changes too. The imagery becomes more coherent and profound. Brilliant insights can arise. Poetry, music, lateral thoughts, extraordinary perspectives on reality can spring up without any ego-involvement on your part. In fact, anything the human mind has ever been capable of can arise in this state. It is the source of all inspiration. You know what the old Indian sages mean when they talk about "the play of consciousness."

Four States of Consciousness

Useful as the hypnagogic state is, there are still deeper states of mind. In the East, there are considered to be four classical stages of "awakening," or the full development of consciousness. These are:

1. being awake while awake
2. being awake while dreaming
3. being awake in dreamless sleep, and
4. integrating all three states at once.

The first state, being awake while awake, means to be fully aware of thoughts, sensations and feeling as they arise. It is the opposite of running on automatic pilot or daydreaming or sleepwalking through life. It is a continuous self-reflective awareness in the beta and alpha states of waking life.

The second state is to be awake in theta, as described above. The third state is to be awake in dreamless sleep, when the brain emits the very slow delta brainwaves. Only the very best meditators can stay conscious in this state. These are the profound depths of trance where there can be consciousness but no "you" at all.

It is a state of unimaginable peace and delight. It is described as being one with God or the cosmos. The Tibetans call it "the pregnant void," or the emptiness from which all things arise. Mystics describe it as the end of the journey. What else could you possibly want?

Its only shortcoming is that it doesn't last. You still have to come back to your toothache and sore back and earn your daily bread. So the ultimate state is to integrate all three states at once, like living in three mutually contradictory realities.

This fourth state is to embody the indescribable bliss of deep trance while arguing with your three-year-old over breakfast. In the deep state, you could watch the destruction of galaxies with equanimity, but in daily life it is important to also have matching socks. If you can integrate all three states, you still go and look for the missing sock.

How Do You Go into Theta?

We go into theta any time we're sleepy. The real question is, how do you consciously enter theta and consciously stay there? The simple answer is that you do what you always do: you focus on one thing and watch other thoughts and sensations with detachment. However, you do this much better than usual.

Meditation is a forgiving practice. Often we don't focus very well, and the mind gets tangled in thoughts. Nonetheless we relax, and the mind feels more settled afterward. However, it takes more than this to stay conscious in theta.

As you go from beta to alpha to theta, the way you perceive the meditation object changes. Your ability to focus changes in stages we could describe as: unfocused, focusing with struggle, focusing without struggle, and absorption.

In beta, your focus is scattered. You can't stay with the object more than a second or two. As you start relaxing, you can focus better, but it's still a struggle. As you settle in, it's much easier to hold the object, and the surrounding thoughts and sensations don't bother you. You're now focusing without struggle.

The less distracted you are, the deeper you go into the object. It looms large in the mind. If you enter and explore it with a kind of lazy curiosity, you may find the background thoughts and sensation vanish altogether for seconds at a time. This is called a state of absorption, or "samadhi," where there is nothing in the mind but the meditation object.

This is the point at which you usually drop into theta. The background thoughts that usually stir you up have been eclipsed. By focusing totally on an object, you've forgotten yourself. You're going into ecstasy (in the sense of "standing outside" yourself).

At this point, you may lose the object, drop into moments of unconsciousness or get distracted by hypnagogic imagery. To stay in control, you have to develop excellent focus, so you know where your mind really is. You also need excellent awareness, so you can notice the imagery without falling in love with it.

Acute moment-to-moment focus is the key that unlocks theta. Personally, I check myself the whole way down. Typically, I focus on the breath to start with and ask, "Did I catch the exact moment that breath stopped?" If my mind is a little turbulent, I can't really be sure.

As my mind settles, I switch to the heartbeat and ask, "Did I catch the very beginning of that beat?" When I'm sharp enough to do that, I then go into the gap between the beats and ask, "What's happening here?"

Interestingly, this is not a dead or empty space. The delicate play of almost invisible sensation here has a rhythmic ebb and flow like all living processes. When my mind is focused enough to notice the rise and fall of these subtle sensations, I know I'm going into theta.

In other words, I use focusing like increasing the magnification on a microscope. I go deeper and deeper into the detail of my object whenever I can. This distances me from thoughts and takes me into a state of absorption.

In this state time can slow right down. The seconds break up into long microseconds. Nonetheless, I rarely settle into high-detail focus for more than a few seconds, without also noticing peripheral things with equal clarity. Absorption and the theta states do not need to obliterate everything else.

You can't force yourself to focus if your mind is turbulent. Until you've acknowledged what's troubling you, it usually won't let you go. Good focus comes not by holding tight to the object but by completely letting go everything else. This often takes time and honesty and there aren't any shortcuts.

Good Awareness

A parallel way to enter theta is to be hyperaware. If you notice the changing landscape as you relax, you can focus on it to take you deeper. If you tune into the physical and mental signs of alpha and theta, they act as biofeedback mechanisms and accelerate the process.

The physical signs that you are entering theta are: the body feeling numb, floating, hollow or vanishing; a great stillness and the breathing almost stopped; very faint sensations of "energy-flow" in your vanishing body.

The mental signs are: moments of oblivion or a sense of emptiness; hypnagogic imagery or irrational thoughts; a sense of extreme detachment or dissociation and an absence of self; and an impersonal happiness or bliss.

To stay in this stage, you need to notice the signs with almost complete indifference. If you get excited and say, "What was that?" you're bound to lose it and shoot back into alpha.

When you are capable of saying "no" to absolutely everything, you are then free to say "yes." You can pluck an image, mood or insight from the stream of consciousness and explore it. Ideally you are quiet and very dispassionate as you do it. You can lose your clear, mirrorlike mind in a flash unless you're vigilant.

Meditation: Inner Space

This is actually a meditation within a meditation. Five or ten minutes into a sitting, when you feel relaxed and lucid, you can consciously go deeper. You do it by increasing the magnification on your microscope. I should add that this won't work unless you've already allowed the background disturbances to clear.

INSTRUCTIONS

- Notice when you are sharp enough to catch the microsecond the breath stops. Also notice exactly where it seems to start.
- Sink into the space between out-breath and in-breath. Don't hurry the new breath.
- In that space, feel the heartbeat.
- Try to catch the exact start and finish of the heartbeat.
- Sink into the space between the beats. Notice the background hum of sensation.

- Notice how those sensations also rise and fall. Try to catch the moment they come and go.
- Now expand your awareness. What else is in consciousness at this moment? (There could be hypnagogic images or what seem to be faint ripples in space.)
- Notice how still the mind and body have become. Enjoy the profound texture of this tranquility.

Visual and Walking Meditations

During the day you see many attractive things—a flowering bush, storm clouds, a bright design on a dress or a book, a play of shadow on the floor. It's easy to focus on one of these for a few seconds longer than you would otherwise.

This kind of spot meditation will slow your mind down, break the momentum of thoughts and increase your sense pleasure. Just thirty seconds is quite enough to drop your tension levels maybe 10 percent. Though brief, this would be a good meditation.

You can also do this more deliberately, as is done in the East. In the instructions below I offer lots of options to play with. What you actually do depends on the object, the amount of time you have and your own temperament. The bottom line is: enjoy what you're looking at and relax.

I usually teach this meditation putting by several objects on a table—some flowers, a candle, a mango, a piece of driftwood, a silk scarf. Some students are interested in none of these and focus instead on the table or the carpet (which are also quite attractive). It is like playtime at kindergarten: I let the kids choose their own toys.

Even a visual object meditation should start with attention to posture, if only for fifteen seconds. I then ask the students to let their eyes roam casually over the objects until something leaps out at them. Once they've made their choice, they let their gaze settle into it.

When you are mentally active, your eyes are continually moving in their sockets. They move faster when you are tense and slower as you relax. It is not surprising that the little eye-swivelling muscles feel tired at the end of a day. This constant eye movement is also what keeps things in your peripheral vision in focus.

Nonetheless, it's quite easy to consciously soften the eyes and let them settle on one thing. This can act as a trigger that softens the whole face. Let the eyes blink as much as they want, so you're not staring.

Now slowly and gently take in your object. Pick up color and shape and texture. Let your eyes go for a lazy stroll over the object and bring up the photographic detail you didn't notice at first. You're not blankly staring in the hope that you'll relax. If someone asked you what your object looked like, you could tell them.

When they do this practice in the East, they sometimes "name" their object. For example, you could say "rose" each time you breathe out. If you're more tuned into the color than the object itself, you could say "red." In fact, you could do both, saying "red" as you breathe in and "rose" as you breathe out.

This connects your body and the object. It's as if you're breathing through it. The words act like an affirmation, reminding you what you are focused on. This device is particularly good if you are in a place with lots of distractions such as a supermarket line.

As you relax and get closer to the dream state, the imagination often comes to the fore. Just as listening to music can raise images and memories, so can looking at an object. You look at a flower and remember your grandmother had similar flowers in her garden. You look at a mango and remember the taste and texture of the last mango you ate.

When I was a child, I used to imagine what an ant would see as it climbed a tree. If you wish, you can imagine climbing over an apple or going inside it. You may look at an odd-shaped rock or wood grain and see an elephant there, or a face looking back at you. If this happens, have fun with it without getting too excited. Meditation should have an element of play about it.

When you relax, you occasionally get optical distortions. Often your peripheral vision goes hazy, you get a tunnel-vision effect or the carpet starts to swirl. This occurs because your eyes are not moving around as they usually do.

The eyes actually have to move slightly for us to see anything at all. If they become utterly still, as can happen in a deep meditation, you actually see nothing at all. You're so tranquil that nothing matters, but a little voice within you asks, "Am I going blind?"

You'll find that focusing on a visual object can relax you very rapidly. It's easy to stay with, and the mind doesn't wander so much. Within three or four minutes, you may find your eyes wanting to close. If you do, you'll realize how relaxed you've become. You're often just one step above sleep.

You can even close your eyes and continue focusing on an object by going over it in your memory. Very few people see it vividly, as if it were projected on a screen, but all can remember something about it. Just saying the words "red rose" as you breathe would be quite enough to keep you focused.

Taking a Snapshot

If you look carefully at anything, you'll find you can bring it to mind later in the day. For example, I can still remember the little white chihuahua I saw as I walked to the supermarket this morning. The usual reason we can't remember things is that we didn't notice them in the first place. Our minds were too cluttered to take in anything else.

I love to meditate for short bursts on visual objects. I call this "taking a snapshot." I aim for a few seconds of total absorption in a leaf, a bird's feather, the bark on a tree, or a shadow on a wall. The "exposure" may only be twenty seconds, but it cuts the other thoughts dead. In those few moments, I've lost myself. I'm just leaf. I'm just chihuahua.

I even do this while walking. I pass a cat on a brick wall and imprint it in my mind. As I walk on I play over the memory of the cat. It is extraordinary how much detail you can catch in a flash.

At the end of the day, it is easy to bring some of those snapshots back. If I am meditating, I can pull one out and focus on it for a few seconds. It is like reliving the loveliest moments of the day. In fact, I can still remember snapshots from years ago.

Taking snapshots like this enhances memory and is a good training ground for visualization. One reason people can't visualize a rose is that they haven't consciously looked at one for years.

In traditional Buddhist training, you would look at a lotus in front of you. You would then close your eyes and picture it. When you lost it, you'd open your eyes to look again, and so on. By the end of the day, you could walk through the forest with the lotus comfortably lodged in your mind.

Meditation: Visual Objects

INSTRUCTIONS

- Spend a few seconds relaxing your body and breathing.
- Settle your eyes on something in front of you and let them soften.
- Slowly and playfully examine your object—color, shape and texture.
- If you want, name the object, the color or both as you breathe.
- If associations arise, weave them in. If your imagination comes into play, enjoy it but don't get too busy.
- If you want, close your eyes and go over the memory of the object.
- Keep a background awareness of your body, to make sure you are actually relaxing.

Walking Meditations

You don't need to sit down to meditate. Almost any meditation you do sitting can also be done walking. And any good meditator should be able to get off his chair or cushion and stay calm and relaxed while walking.

Walking meditations have an ancient history. That they're largely ignored now is sad. Perhaps this is because few Western teachers have been thoroughly trained, and most Asian teachers are too encumbered by religion to be good meditation instructors.

Even good meditators assume that if an hour of sitting meditation is good, then eight hours is that much better. In fact, too much of a good thing turns it into a bad thing. Too much sitting can lead to inertia, excessive introspection and an unwillingness to face the challenges of life. It's rarely good for people with depression, for example.

If we only think of meditation as the deep tranquil state we get while sitting, then we can't integrate it into our lives. Our physiology changes when we start moving. This doesn't mean we're stressed, but the feeling is not like the low metabolic state of sitting. We can still be calm and clear while active, even though it has a different quality—usually more awake.

For some people, walking is by far the best way to meditate. It particularly suits those who are young, mentally active or highly stressed or anxious. For these people, sitting still just doesn't feel right. They can force themselves to do it, but they'd do much better walking.

An Ancient and Versatile Tradition

If you sit to meditate, all your worries can jump on you. Once you close your eyes, you may find yourself caught in thought from start to finish. You may find it much easier to shift from thinking to sensing by taking a dawn stroll by the river or an evening ramble through the back streets.

Walking takes you into neutral territory. You can metaphorically walk away from home, work and responsibilities and leave them behind you. Walking simplifies things. You can't do much when you walk. But it does put you in touch with yourself, your body and the natural world.

Without knowing it, you are imitating the Indian holy men of old. Most of them weren't monks. The monasteries came much later.

They were "wanderers," or "homeless ones," who brushed the dust of city life from their feet and roamed all their lives.

Walking is as ancient a meditation posture as sitting. Australian Aborigines go "walkabout." Native Americans go on spirit quests. Young men and women of all times leave the cozy certainties of home to find themselves. Walking reminds us of our nomadic ancestry when we owned nothing and faced each day afresh. A simple life.

The Buddha encouraged his students to spend no more than three days in one place (except during the rainy season). So they walked a lot, and developed walking into a deliberate practice.

Over the years, these simple practices became elaborate and formal. Burmese monks may walk extremely slowly, verbally noting each micro-movement of the feet. It can take half an hour to cross the room, walking like this. Though not that relaxing, it can make the mind exceptionally sharp.

Zen practitioners may walk in a circle, synchronizing their steps. Kung Fu and Tai Chi are elaborate versions of the Buddhist and Taoist walking and standing meditations.

On some ten-day retreats, people alternate sitting and walking meditations. It is traditional to walk slowly back and forth on a path about twenty yards long. Sitting and walking complement each other well. Sitting makes you calm but a little dull. Walking makes you sharp but is not so relaxing. So you walk to wake up and sit to settle down.

Yet I think that ordinary walking, like ordinary breathing, is best. It's also versatile. You can meditate any time you're on your feet—going to the shops, through the park, in a crowded street. Since you can't do much else while you walk, why don't you take it easy and get the mind clear?

Softening the Eyes

Obviously when you walk you notice people, curbs, cars, trees, sky and birds. Your eyes usually hop from attraction to attraction like summer flies. If your eyes move too quickly, you won't relax much. You need to slow down the eye movements.

There are several ways to do this. In all of them, the eyes will be active enough to stop you bumping into strangers and tripping over curbs. First you could hook them on a point in the distance—a car or tree—like casting a fishing line, and reel yourself toward it. This helps you resist glancing sideways. When you get too close, cast your eyes over something else.

Second, you could look at the ground a few yards ahead so you see where you're going but not much else. This makes you look quite serious and even pious.

Third, you can let your eyes glaze over slightly. Let them rest back in their sockets and half-close the lids. Try to evoke the way the eyes feel as you come out of a sitting meditation: soft and gentle and even a little out of focus.

One problem with walking meditations is that they're too pleasant. Because you feel good, you forget they're a discipline to help you withdraw from thoughts. There are lots of distractions anyway, so you're inclined to let the mind drift. Soon you're just walking in the park, with your usual mental cocktail of thoughts and feelings.

There are a few things that can help. It's good to be grounded in the body, even if you're primarily focused on something external. Also, encourage the mind to slow down. Although it's okay to shift your focus, unless you stay with each object for at least ten seconds the meditation never gets going.

The boundaries between these meditations can easily blur. Make sure it doesn't get too mushy. Know what it is you're doing and stick to it, for a few minutes at least, before you shift your focus.

It also helps to practice each individual meditation once a day for four consecutive days. This is what takes you beyond the initial awkwardness and engraves the practice in long-term memory. Otherwise walking meditations will be little more than a nice idea that you dabble with occasionally.

There are a huge variety of walking meditations. In the examples below, you'll notice that the first three have you focusing inward, on the body and the breathing. The later ones have you focusing outward, on the sense world around you.

Meditation: Walking Comfortably

An old Buddhist aphorism goes, "When walking, just walk." In other words, focus on the sensations of the moving body and pull away from random thoughts.

If you are anxious, you walk anxiously. You can see it in any city street. People walk with a stiff gait, hunched shoulders, tight breathing and blank eyes. Their anxieties are mirrored in their gait.

If you pay attention to how you are walking, you'll soon find yourself walking more comfortably. In this meditation, your aim is to walk with no excess tension. The body should feel balanced and open. It can help to scan the body up and down as you walk, allowing the movement to free up tensions. You could say a mantra or the words, "walking easily," in time with your steps, if you wish.

The body enjoys moving. It is a lovely rhythmic action. Parents use it to soothe their babies. It moves the juices along and keeps muscles and brain alive. If we are too sedentary, the muscles atrophy and the mind feels dull. If we stop moving altogether, parts of the body start dying, and that doesn't feel good at all.

Movement is also the obvious way to release tension. The fight-or-flight response is firing up the body for action. This is why when you're under extreme stress, you unwind better by being active than by sitting. It's what the body wants to do anyway. Sitting still can just make the muscles lock up further.

Walking is rhythmic, and anything rhythmic stimulates the alpha brainwaves. The hips and shoulders swing easily. The breathing may synchronize with the footsteps. The continuous ripple of sensations can massage muscles made tight by too much sitting or thinking.

When walking you'll still be subject to distractions. The usual principles apply: focus on your object (in this case, the body), and watch other thoughts and sensations with detachment. When you find you've "jumped the fence," name the distraction and return to the body.

Meditation: Counting the Steps

If you've burst out of the office at the end of the day with your mind in chaos, you'll need a very crude and obvious meditation object or you'll lose it. In this case, count your footsteps. This meditation may seem rather silly, but it is an excellent emergency measure.

Since we can all count automatically, make the counting more complex to stay with it. Walk at your usual pace but first count from one to five steps, then one to six steps, then one to seven and one to eight. Then back to one to five. So the meditation goes "1,2,3,4, five! 1,2,3,4,5,six! 1,2,3,4,5,6,seven! 1,2,3,4,5,6,7,eight!" And so on.

You have to pay attention to do this, or you'll soon find you're up to fifteen. Within a minute or two, you'll find you've stopped thinking about work and realize, "It's quite a nice day out here!"

Meditation: The Breath

In this meditation, synchronize your breathing and footsteps, the way runners often do. You find out roughly how many steps you take as you breathe in, and roughly how many steps you take out, and set that up as a pattern. The out-breath is usually a little longer than the in-breath.

Mentally count the steps. You may count three steps as you breathe in and four as you breathe out. Or you may have a two-three rhythm or a five-five rhythm. Just do what feels natural. If the rhythm changes as you continue to walk, then change the count.

Meditation: Random Sounds

The three practices above all focus you inward on your body and the breath. Nonetheless, by extracting you from thoughts they'll automatically enhance your awareness of your surroundings. It's always good to get grounded in the body first, but you can also meditate on external things such as sounds, sights, smells or all three at once.

If you are meditating on sounds, the art is to highlight or hold on to each one for several seconds at least. This is what slows the mind down. If you skim too quickly from sensation to sensation, you'll soon skim back into thought.

So actively focus on sounds and linger with each one, while passively noticing the other sensations. It's not that the other sensations are bad, or distractions that have to be avoided. It's just that deeper focus slows the mind down and is more satisfying.

Meditation: Visual Objects

When you walk, there are hundreds of visual objects that can catch your eyes. As with sounds, the meditation won't work if you let the mind skim rapidly from one to another. You'll fail to make genuine contact with any one of them. In other words, you won't really bring it into focus.

So as you walk, let your eyes go from tree to sky to grass to sidewalk, but do it slowly. Linger with each one at least ten to fifteen seconds. Don't go looking for something new. Wait with one thing till something else grabs you. It's even better if you return to the body or the breath between each object. That will keep you grounded. You could also do the "Snapshot" meditation that was mentioned in the last lesson.

Meditation: Wind

This ancient practice is quite delicious. You focus on the movement of air over your body as you walk or even sit outside. Even on a still day, the air masses shift around you, touching your cheek, neck or leg in succession. This is a very sensual practice. It feels like the earth is breathing over you. It's quite passive, like listening to sounds. You just wait for the next lick of air on your skin.

Meditation: Being Present

In this practice, focus on whatever sensation catches your attention in the moment. What makes this different from a stroll in the park is that you linger with each one until something else replaces it. You sink into the detail: the smell of the earth, the sight of birds fighting, a blast of wind in your ear, the crunch of gravel underfoot. It's still a discipline. You notice when you're lost and return to the present.

Meditations: Space and Light

Say the word "space" as you take in the feeling of the sky above you. Internalize it. Imagine space flowing through your body.

Alternatively, you could focus on light. Notice the quality of light wherever you see it. Don't focus on the trees so much as the light sparkling through them. Notice the light shining off a window rather than the window itself. Once again, you can internalize the light, so you feel it shining within you.

Imagery, Visualization and Being Present

You can use an image just like any meditation object: you focus on it and, when the mind wanders off, you return to it. Using an image or a visualization in this way can work just as well as using the breath or a mantra.

The simplest images usually take you deepest. You may find the breath boring to watch, but you can easily imagine your child's face, a rose, a rainbow or a scene in the country. In fact, focusing on something imaginary may work better for you than something "real."

Meditation works because it is so simple. However, people often visualize for quite complicated purposes. They want to heal themselves or change negative thought patterns or contact spirit guides or picture their future. While useful, the effort and striving involved can work against the desire for a calm, clear mind. I'll discuss these practices later in the chapter.

What Exactly Is a Visualization?

People often complain that they can't visualize, but that's equivalent to saying they have no memory. They are misunderstanding what the term actually means. Try this little exercise and see what happens:

Imagine an apple. What kind is it? Red Delicious? Granny Smith? Big or small? Feel its weight and texture in your hand. Is it smooth or waxy or slightly sticky?

Imagine biting into it. Feel the resistance of the skin before it breaks. Is it crisp or a little soft? Notice the first burst of smell and taste. Hear the sound as you bite off a piece, and feel it moving around your mouth. Imagine swallowing it.

This exercise undoubtedly evoked something in you—an image, memory or sensation at least. Maybe you started salivating. Maybe the visuals weren't strong but other sensations were. I doubt that you got nothing at all.

"Visualization" is an unsatisfactory term. The exercise above evoked all five senses. A better term would be "sensualization." The emphasis on visuals is unfortunate. Jose Silva, the grandfather of American mind-training gurus, suggests you project an image onto a mental screen in front of you. I find only about 20 percent of people can do this. It's a genetic endowment, like blue eyes.

Many more of us have a "kinesthetic" imagination. We "see" things via feeling or mood and can as easily evoke sound, touch, smell or taste. Our "visualizations" commonly evoke the whole multisensual experience. We can imagine a friend's dog, for example—the long fur, the snuffly mouth in your ear, the romping energy—without the visuals being particularly clear. How did you do with the apple? Which was the strongest sensation?

Read the following sequence slowly. Give each image and its associated mood a few seconds to arise. Notice which of the senses is strongest. Notice if your body responds to individual images. It's possible that your body may relax or recoil, for example. Linger on the images that grab you. I am sure some will catch your attention more than others:

- a melting ice cream cone
- a sharp pain
- the feel of wind on your face

- the smell of gas
- being in bed with your partner
- a flowering bush
- a baby's skin
- a dead animal on the road
- being at the beach
- your grandmother

The images that worked best for you probably weren't just pictures. They also evoked feeling and a response in the body. In other words, your body reacted as if you were actually there. If you imagine being under a cold shower, you literally feel your skin contracting. If you then imagine basking in the sun, you feel it expanding. If you are meditating for healing, for example, this body response and emotional tone is much more important than clear visuals.

Where Do I Want to Be?

If you feel tired, sick and miserable, it is useful to meditate in a way that picks up your spirits. This is when it's good to focus on something pleasant such as music or a beautiful visualization.

Sometimes you just need a holiday, so give yourself one. You don't have to wait till Christmas. You can go to the mountains or to Africa in your mind. I like to tailor these escapist fantasies to my exact mood. I ask myself, "Where would I like to be right now?" and wait for the images to arise.

These are often quite precise and different each time. Perhaps I want to sit under the hanging branches of a tree at dusk in autumn with evening mist around the hills. Maybe I want to be in the Arctic tundra in midsummer, or perhaps with my friend in New Zealand, having a cup of tea on his verandah.

In a good visualization, each detail is like a holograph and contains the emotion of the whole. It's better to go deep into single details than to paint an entire picture. Imagine the smell of damp earth or the squawk of distant birds or the steam swirling from the teacup warm in your hands. Be simple and let the mind slow down. Planning the itinerary for a trip through Europe won't have the same effect.

Programmed Visualizations

There are two distinct approaches to visualizing. In the first, you "make" the image appear. You program it. In the second, you "allow" or "invite" the image to arise of its own accord. Programming takes place in the beta and alpha states. Inviting usually occurs in the alpha and theta states.

An example of programming would be to imagine the colors of the rainbow in the seven chakras of the body. An example of inviting would be to go into each chakra and ask, "Is there a color or an image here?"

People usually prefer one approach over the other. One man told me he could even program his dreams. However, the idea of allowing images to arise freely was repugnant to him.

The Western tradition emphasizes programming the mind. St. Ignatius, the founder of the Jesuit order, said we should evoke images that make us better Christians. For example, you could imagine being in Nazareth talking to Jesus and taking advice from him. St. Ignatius regarded meditation as "an exercise of the will" to enhance the good and repress bad instincts.

Similarly, the American thought-control schools train people to imagine themselves confident, successful and achieving their goals. The idea here is that thoughts have an almost magical effect if you can control them. In other words, what you think or believe, good or bad, will come true.

Obviously, there is a grain of truth in this. People who whine and complain a lot are rarely happy. Conversely, people who have a well-balanced optimism often get along very nicely in life. But this idea can be taken to an absurd degree.

I recently received a panicky call from a woman with cancer. "I've got to stop every negative thought," she said. "How can I do it?" Any meditator could tell her she was attempting the impossible. We can't dominate our thoughts this way. They have a will of their own. Nor is it good to regard our spontaneous thoughts as potentially evil. It's what we do with them afterward that is the problem.

In the West, meditation has strong overlaps with conscious thought. After all, the literal meaning of the word "meditate" is "to think deeply" about something. It's a pity that the same word is applied to the nonverbal practices I describe in this book. It is best to regard programmed visualizations as a kind of deep thinking but a shallow meditation.

If you meditate with a sense of "I want this to happen," it will keep you out of the transpersonal states where the sense of "I" dissolves. Useful as these practices are, they lack the passive, accepting, effortless quality of most meditations.

Spontaneous Visualizations

The shift from beta to alpha to theta is a shift from thinking to sensing to imagery. As you relax, sensations and images naturally replace the words in your mind. Once you are in alpha, it can be quite easy to evoke images and sensations.

Most people find it easier to work with images that arise freely or with whatever comes up. You may not be able to picture a perfect white rose and fix it like a photograph to a wall. But if you put in a request, the mind will deliver something. A daisy or camellia may come up instead. And it may be pink or yellow rather than white. Perhaps it is fully open and past its prime. There may be some bruising on the outer petals. And there is a bug inside . . .

As you enter theta, hypnagogic imagery can arise without your even asking for it. This tends to be too speedy to focus on for long, but some images last longer than others. You can pluck one of them out of the stream and hold it gently in your hands. If it wriggles too much, let it go.

In theta, the sense of self is very faint. Nonetheless, it is possible to ask for an image while in theta. What arises is often powerful and unexpected, coming as it does from the dream mind.

Finding the Image Stream

It may interest you to know how I learned to visualize. In my initial training I was encouraged to focus purely on physical sensation. I was taught to ignore images as being distractions and "not real."

I felt that something was lacking, however, so I took up the Tibetan practices. My training involved literally tens of thousands of prostrations, mantras and accompanying visualizations. This was not at all what I thought of as meditation.

Even worse, after years of ignoring images, I now found myself apparently unable to visualize at all. I sympathize completely with students who say, "I can't see anything when I try to visualize!" I was trying to visualize deities, colors, trees, crystal palaces, animals, jewels, energy flows in the body, and I was getting nothing at all.

Yet I doggedly persisted and quite suddenly, early one morning, it happened. It was like a door flying open. The imagery had always been there. I just hadn't looked in the right direction. The images didn't compete with or replace reality. They were like a superimposition, or double image, overlaying it.

Once I knew how to look, the image bank opened. Memories arose in extraordinary detail from my childhood and youth. With this vast picture library available to me, I found visualizing an easy practice.

For one whole month, I mentally returned for a few minutes each day to my childhood home to see what else I could remember from that time. I never got to the end of it. A few years later, I was even able to check whether the details were correct. The house was rented out to students by this time, and they were quite happy to let me go right through it. I wasn't far wrong.

Now when I meditate, I often have a quiet trickle of polysensual images in the background. Occasionally, it erupts into a cacophony like a Hollywood blockbuster. At other times it almost vanishes. It seems that some part of my mind is always dreaming, day and night, even as I eat breakfast, answer the telephone and work on the computer. It is where imagination and that part of us that thinks in metaphors come from.

Over the years, the quality of the images has changed. The parade of images from youth, childhood and infancy has largely finished. They now seem to arise from a place beyond my personal history. It may come from what the psychologist Jung called "the collective unconscious." Much of it, I am sure, is what is known as "cryptomnesia"—the ability of the mind to invent strong images from sources in long-forgotten books and movies.

It seems our minds are continually generating polysensual imagery that we just don't notice because our minds are too busy with thoughts. These images are like the stars in the sky. We don't see them when the sun is out. We only notice them when dreaming or at the edge of sleep.

Where Am I? What Is This?

A dream, or inner imagery, is often a comment on how we feel at the moment. It generally tells us what is out of balance, and we don't have to go to sleep to hear these messages.

Recently I put the phone down after an amicable conversation but felt awful. So I asked, "What is this?" (Or, to ask it another way, "What does this feel like?")

The image soon came. It was as if I had eaten moldy fruitcake. (The unconscious has a great sense of humor!) The image brought some insight also. The woman I spoke to had great ability (the richness of the fruitcake) that was flawed by her manipulative nature (the mold). The image told me how I was instinctively responding to her.

So Many Ways to Visualize

Most meditations are clear and logical practices. Visualizing, however, is very idiosyncratic. There is no one way to do it. Just as some people never dream and others dream all night, the way people work with their imaginations is as personal as can be.

Furthermore, visualizing is rarely a "pure" practice. Meditation, as I explain it in this book, is designed to simplify and clear the mind—a return to the essence of consciousness. Visualization, however, naturally blends with thinking, imaginative invention, therapy, fantasy and religious and philosophic beliefs. It's a kind of pure meditation *plus* whatever you like.

Unfortunately, people who actively visualize for whatever purpose tend to neglect the "calm body, clear mind" aspects of meditation. Such people commonly focus on the breath or the body for just a minute or two, using it as an antechamber to their visualizations. In their enthusiasm for inspiration they may ignore the mundane spade work that keeps the wellspring open.

It doesn't have to be this way. If you relax into the theta state and lay a strong foundation of physical calm and mental clarity, your imagery will draw from the depths of the unconscious. It really can become a dialogue with God or the hidden powers of the mind.

A minority of people have strong visual imaginations. When they meditate, they are bound to use this ability. It would be hard for them to put it aside. Being imaginative anyway, they will develop or adopt visualizations that particularly suit them. This kind of person doesn't need a lot of help with visualization.

Guided Visualizations

Guided meditations that take you on a journey can be a lot of fun. For some people, and particularly for children, they are ideal. Of course, they tend to depend on someone talking you through them.

The common ingredients in many of them are excellent metaphors of meditation itself. You are alone (i.e., you come back to yourself). You descend a staircase (i.e., you go deep within). You walk (i.e., you walk away from your concerns) into a beautiful landscape (which is sensual and grounding).

These practices often give opportunities for images to arise spontaneously. You go into a garden and what do you see? You open a box and what is there? You see a wise man and what do you ask him? And what does he say? If your mind is passive and open, the results can be very illuminating.

Before you finish, it's useful to choose a single image from the scene to remind you of it. This can act as a talisman later. You can recall the image and it will partly reawaken the feeling of the meditation.

Keeping It Simple

Most people will be more moderate in their use of imagery. Since images occur naturally when you're relaxed and at the edge of sleep, why not use them? Here are some ways to use images while still calming the body and clearing the mind.

If an image arises in a meditation, use it as a temporary point of focus, just as you could with a sound or a pain. Don't get all excited and ask, "What does this mean?" Just examine it dispassionately, noting its sensual qualities of color, shape and texture, as you would with a flower or a candle in front of you. Let the image go as soon as it fades and return to your original focus.

While you focus on the breath or the body, you can also imagine some familiar object—an apple, a cat, a tree. You could even put one of these in front of you and open and close your eyes throughout the meditation. Or you could focus on some clear image from memory.

You could imagine places. Your living room, the walk to work, a friend's house, a familiar park or beach would work well. You could just imagine the view out your window. Or you could imagine a completely imaginary place. One of my students was an anxious and depressed real estate salesman. The only way he could meditate at all was to go through every house he had ever sold.

You could imagine color. Traditionally, you would try to evoke a single color for several days before moving to the next. To focus on "yellow" for example, you could consciously notice all the yellow things you see during the day. You'd then find it easy to imagine the color when you sit to meditate.

Colors are usually easier to imagine if linked with objects. You could go through the spectrum imagining in turn a red tomato, an orange orange, a yellow daffodil, a green leaf, the blue of the sky and so on.

You can add color when you scan your body. For example, you could gradually fill your body with blue or gold light. Or you could imagine the seven colors of the spectrum radiating from the seven chakras. Or you could go to any place in your body and ask, "what's your color?," or "what color would you like?"

Visualization

BASIC INSTRUCTIONS

- Focus on the breath or the body as usual.
- When relaxed and clear, invite an image to arise.
- Gently explore the sensory detail. Let its mood wash through you.
- If you wish, you can "name" it as you breathe.
- If it starts to fade, ask, "Is there another image there?"
- Periodically check your body to see if you're actually relaxing.
- Be quite prepared to let the image go and return to the breath.

Being Present

A Zen master was asked, "How often do you meditate?" He answered, "When am I not meditating?" Obviously he understood the question differently from the questioner. Even a master must eat and go to the toilet, gets angry and sad occasionally, has to deal with difficult people, sickens and dies. Can he "meditate" through all that?

To be honest, he probably can't, but the ideal is worth keeping in mind. It should be possible to accept the pleasure and pain of life just as it is, without stressing out about it as well. I haven't found that Zen practitioners are especially serene, but they're certainly willing to face the moment fully.

If one word describes meditation, it is "awareness." This means being awake while awake, or being attuned to what is happening in the moment. St. Theresa was once criticized for eating perch with obvious gusto. She said, "When I pray, I pray. When I eat fish, I eat fish." She doesn't eat fish trying to look as if she were praying. Being relaxed means being in harmony with the situation you are in. It may be a calm or busy, enjoyable or stressful situation. If you're not at ease with it, the problem (and the solution) is not "out there." It is in you.

Formal meditation is just square one. It is practice, not the real thing. After all, meditation is tranquil. Life isn't, and we can't run from life forever. It has a habit of muscling in the door. Meditation should be a preparation for life, not an escape from it. The secret is to weave the stillness and detachment of meditation into the turbulence of your day.

First you find you can remain relaxed and alert with your eyes open. Then while walking in the park or on the beach. Then while doing simple activities such as preparing a meal or having a shower.

Soon you find you can stay calm when someone presses your buttons. Boring tasks become less irksome. You appreciate moments of beauty in the midst of turmoil and have moments of clarity even in strong emotion. This is the art of being relaxed and alert in the present.

Being Calm and Clear in All Circumstances

Beginners often have little flexibility at first. They say, "I couldn't meditate because . . .":

- a dog was barking
- I could hear the TV next door
- I had a stomachache
- I've got too much on my mind
- I'm angry with my ex-husband
- It was a long day. I am too tired

Eventually they realize it is all grist for the mind. Such obstructions are opportunities to passively notice and accept the things that can't be changed anyway. Meditation doesn't magically dispel the pain and take you into bliss. It only enables you to find the point of balance. A meditator doesn't calm the waves. He or she just floats like a cork on the ups and downs.

The way to stay afloat is to stay awake, but this goes against the grain of our habits. We tend to operate on automatic pilot. We can shuffle through the day not sensing or feeling anything clearly. What is worse, we can be too distracted to realize it. Some days, we're just not here at all.

Operating on automatic does give the mind a break. It is restful, but it blurs the perception of reality and so is a mixed blessing. Just because we wake up in the morning doesn't mean we are fully here.

Many of us choose to be more or less unaware. Instead of being right here, we switch on the TV or read the paper. Often it takes an illness like cancer to make people wake up. Such people say they suddenly see what is important—feeling the dawn air, walking around the garden, sharing a moment with a friend.

Awareness doesn't come automatically. If you want to be relaxed and in balance amid the ups and downs, it helps to practice it. The best way to start is to be present. This means noticing the sights, sounds, smells, tastes and tactile sensations of the moment.

Making Simple Activities into Meditations

This is kitchen-sink meditation. I often meditate while preparing food. Sometimes I focus on one sense, such as sound. I listen to each sound I make: cutting the apple, putting the knife down, the squeal of the tap, the water running, the bowl scraping on the bench, a foot shuffling, the fridge door opening, the clang as I place something on a rack and so on. I hold my mind to the task by saying the word "sound" silently each time I breathe out. I am aware of other sensations, of course, but I highlight the sounds.

Or I notice input from any sense. The texture of the knife, fruit, water, the door handle. The glistening skin of a capsicum, patterns of light and shadow, a stain on the bench. The sensations in my arm as I lift something. I nonverbally ask myself, "Where is my mind right now?" It is amazing how rapidly the mind can disappear into thought, and how interesting the sense world can be if we focus on it.

The Japanese tea ceremony is a multisensory meditation. As the guest, you watch each movement of the tea maker. You enjoy the room, hear the sounds, watch the steam, feel and look at the bowl, taste the tea and feel yourself swallowing. You become tranquil by focusing on one minute detail after another.

The Buddha said, "When walking, just walk. When eating, just eat. Similarly when standing, sitting, getting dressed or going to the toilet." Our problem is that when walking, we think about work. At work, we think about sex. When with our lover or spouse we think about last night's TV. When watching TV, we also eat, read the newspaper and talk to someone. It is not surprising the mind gets confused and exhausted and we don't enjoy the TV, the food or making love as much as we could.

Another Zen master said, "Miraculous activity!—chopping wood and drawing water." If we can't find happiness in this very moment, where will we find it? We are often tense because we always want to be somewhere else, doing something different.

Because being present seems like a good idea, you may resolve, "Today I am going to live in the present!" However, it is better to be more modest with your goals. Don't try to be present for an hour or a day. Just try for a few seconds or minutes at a time. Aim for high quality and short duration.

It can be surprisingly satisfying. Try to eat a cookie consciously. Enjoy watering your plants. Brush your teeth deliberately. Each of these can be very pleasant simply because other thoughts remain backstage and the mind feels comfortable doing one thing at a time.

This kind of meditation has no boundaries. It doesn't require a quiet room and half an hour carved out of the day. Anywhere and any-time will do. You could make any of the following into a meditation.

1.HANGING OUT THE WASH

Feel the wet cloth, the varying weights, the clothespins, the wind on your face, the body sensations of bending and stretching, catching glimpses of the sky . . .

2.GETTING DRESSED OR UNDRESSED

Body movement, texture of the clothing, the sounds of cloth against skin . . .

3.TAKING A SHOWER

Smell of soap, sound of the water, pleasure, warmth, wet skin, the texture of the towel, dry stimulated skin . . .

4.WALKING TO THE SUPERMARKET

Parking the car, turning off the ignition, sounds of opening and closing, walking across the lot, noticing the sky and the trees, shaking the shopping cart loose . . .

Meditation: Being Present

This meditation gives you license to move from one sensory object to another as they come to mind. Even though you're not staying with just one thing, the sensations keep you in the present, as long as you stay with each one for at least ten seconds.

You could move serially from object to object. Or you could multi-layer your meditation by focusing primarily on the breath or the body and adding in new things as they arise.

INSTRUCTIONS

• Sit down and relax the body and breathing as usual.

- Notice what is the strongest sensation and focus on it. It could be the breath, or a pain in the shoulder, or a lawn mower outside.
- Let your mind sink into it. Explore the detail.
- Don't hold the object tightly. If something else catches your attention—a passing car, an itch—shift your focus to that, and so on.
- Check yourself occasionally. Ask "Am I in the present?" or "Where is the mind right now?"
- Check that the body is actually relaxing.

Index

Other Ulysses Press Mind/Body Titles

HOW MEDITATION HEALS: A Scientific Explanation
Eric Harrison, $12.95
In straightforward, practical terms, *How Meditation Heals* reveals how and why meditation improves the natural functioning of the human body.

**HERBS THAT WORK:
The Scientific Evidence of Their Healing Powers**
David Armstrong, $12.95
Unlike herb books relying on folklore or vague anecdotes, *Herbs that Work* is the first consumer guide to rate herbal remedies based on documented, state-of-the-art scientific research.

**SIMPLY RELAX:
An Illustrated Guide to Slowing Down and Enjoying Life**
Dr. Sarah Brewer, $15.95
In a beautifully illustrated format, this book clearly presents physical and mental disciplines that show readers how to relax.

**HOW TO MEDITATE:
An Illustrated Guide to Calming the Mind
and Relaxing the Body**
Paul Roland, $16.95
Offers a friendly, illustrated approach to calming the mind and raising consciousness through various techniques, including basic meditation, visualization, body scanning for tension, affirmations and mantras.

KNOW YOUR BODY: The Atlas of Anatomy
2nd edition, Introduction by Emmet B. Keeffe, M.D., $14.95
Provides a comprehensive, full-color guide to the human body.

**THE JOSEPH H. PILATES METHOD AT HOME:
A Balance, Shape, Strength & Fitness Program**
Eleanor McKenzie, $16.95
This handbook describes and details Pilates, a mental and physical program that combines elements of yoga and classical dance.

PILATES WORKBOOK:
Illustrated Step-by-Step Guide to Matwork Techniques
Michael King, $12.95
Illustrates the core matwork movements exactly as Joseph Pilates
intended them to be performed; readers learn each movement by
following the photographic sequences and explanatory captions.

SENSES WIDE OPEN:
The Art & Practice of Living in Your Body
Johanna Putnoi, $14.95
Through simple, accessible exercises, this book shows how to be
at ease with yourself and experience genuine pleasure in your
physical connection to others and the world.

THE 7 HEALING CHAKRAS:
Unlocking Your Body's Energy Centers
Dr. Brenda Davies, $14.95
Explores the essence of chakras, vortices of energy that connect the
physical body with the spiritual.

101 SIMPLE WAYS TO MAKE YOUR HOME & FAMILY
SAFE IN A TOXIC WORLD
Beth Ann Petro Roybal, $9.95
Sheds light on common toxins found around the house and
offers parents straightforward ways to protect themselves and their
children.

WEEKEND HOME SPA: Four Creative Escapes—
Cleansing, Energizing, Relaxing and Pampering
Linda Bird, $16.95
Shows how to create that spa experience in your own home with
step-by-step mini workouts, stretching routines, meditations and
visualizations, as well as more challenging exercises to boost
mental potential.

To order these books call 800-377-2542 or 510-601-8301, fax 510-601-8307,
e-mail ulysses@ulyssespress.com, or write to Ulysses Press, P.O. Box 3440,
Berkeley, CA 94703. All retail orders are shipped free of charge. California
residents must include sales tax. Allow two to three weeks for delivery.

About the Author

Trained in the Buddhist traditions of Burma and Tibet, Eric Harrison has practiced meditation for more than thirty years. After one particularly intensive retreat, Harrison was encouraged by the monks to begin teaching meditation to others "in his own way." Over the years he has developed a method adapted to Western culture, one that eschews mysticism while emphasizing meditation's practical effects. As the director of Perth Meditation Centre, Harrison has worked closely with local doctors and patients to develop appropriate meditation programs for particular ailments. He lives in Perth, Australia.